THE FILMS OF
BURT REYNOLDS

THE FILMS OF
BURT
REYNOLDS

by Nancy Streebeck

CITADEL PRESS • Secaucus, N.J.

FIRST EDITION
Copyright © 1982 by Nancy Streebeck
All rights reserved
Published by Citadel Press
A division of Lyle Stuart Inc.
120 Enterprise Ave., Secaucus, N.J. 07094

In Canada: Musson Book Company
A division of General Publishing Co. Limited
Don Mills, Ontario

Manufactured in the United States of America by
Halliday Lithograph, West Hanover, Mass.

Library of Congress Cataloging in Publication Data
Streebeck, Nancy.
  The films of Burt Reynolds.

  1. Reynolds, Burt. 2. Moving-picture actors and
actresses—United States—Biography.
I. Title.
PN2287.R447S8   791.43'028'0924 [B]   81-15546
ISBN 0-8065-0785-3   AACR2

To Burt,
who made it happen for a lot
of us.
With love,

N.S.

ACKNOWLEDGEMENTS

The Academy of Motion Picture Arts and Sciences; Robert Aldrich; Peter Bankers, Paramount Pictures; John Boorman; Stanley Brossette; Dick Clayton; Tom Conroy, Movie Still Archives; Watson B. Duncan III; Marty Ingels; Steve Marry, Paramount Pictures; Patrick Miller, 20th Century-Fox; Melinda Mullen; Hal Needham; Fern and Burton Reynolds; Renee Valente; Orson Welles; all of the newspapers and periodicals who graciously permitted me to reprint their words; all of the motion picture, production, and distribution companies who generously researched and provided stills.

Numerous quotes—in part and in full—contained in *The Films of Burt Reynolds* originally appeared in a 1974 *Chicago Tribune* article written by Gene Siskel. The quotes are used with permission, for which the author extends sincere appreciation and gratitude.

CONTENTS

FOREWORD
by Orson Welles

A POPULAR FAVORITE OF Burt Reynolds' magnitude is not always a favorite with the cinema snobs. Blinded by his blazing commercial success, they find it hard to take him seriously as an artist. They should consult their history books. Some of our finest actors have managed to survive the stigma of being Number One at the box office. With Burt, the glamour, the good looks and the charm are the blessings of bankability—not a substitute for talent.

No performer can stand still: he gets better or he gets worse. A dedicated professional, Burt is polishing his skills and getting better all the time, revealing a range and sensitivity which are confounding his critics and surprising even his friends. As a director, he has already made a smashing start in a career which nothing can slow down except the career of the superstar. Success is Burt Reynolds' only handicap.

O.W.

9

INTRODUCTION

BURT REYNOLDS' unquestionable and frequently documented popularity—including being honored as Favorite Motion Picture Actor by *Photoplay* in 1973, 1977, and 1978; Favorite Motion Picture Actor by the People's Choice poll in 1978 and 1979; Top Money-Making Star by U.S. Film Distributors in 1978, 1979, and 1980; and Male Star of the Year by the National Association of Theatre Owners in 1978 and 1980—initially took hold with the release of John Boorman's quality film classic, *Deliverance*, in 1972.

Prior to *Deliverance*, Mr. Reynolds appeared in eleven motion pictures. Most of them were forgettable. The same need not be said of the actor.

"Yes," Burt concedes, "*Deliverance* was my deliverance, but before that I didn't just crawl out from under a fan magazine. I paid my dues. I've always believed that the only way you can get better as an actor is to act. I've done a lot of not-so-wonderful films, but I've done a lot of work I'm proud of, too."

Throughout an offering of early cinematic endeavors, all of which were financially successful, Burt tackled the movie business in an intuitive, subliminal manner that gradually set him entirely apart from other thespians. Coupled with on-the-job training, he honed an inherent "x quality" into big bucks and the big time.

Even now it is difficult to pinpoint this special quality. Ask a dozen Burt watchers and you'll get a dozen different answers—physical appeal, arrogant charm, comedic timing, relaxed virility, energetic magnetism, man-on-the-street identity—a clever, calculating diamond-in-the-rough; a happy, carefree regular fellow.

It is surely a combination of all these things, within a man who constantly strives to make all the elements jell, that singles him out among superstars both past and present.

The former football hero who, with the assistance of friends and associates, has carefully molded his personality into a five-million-dollar commodity, declares, "People say to me, 'There was always a spark there. I always knew you were going to make it.' Nobody knew. There was no hint of anything."

A seemingly honest and introspective comment, but not one that relatives or childhood acquaintances accept as gospel. In fact, the record seems to indicate that Burt has been compelled to excel, whatever the unorthodox route, for nearly half a century. Being number one has always motivated him.

Official biographies designate Burton Leon Reynolds' birthplace as Waycross, Georgia, on February 11, 1936. His mother Fern, a former nurse, and his father Burton, an ex-cowboy turned law officer, resided in several Midwestern and Southern cities before settling down in Riviera Beach, Florida, during the early Forties.

Called "Buddy" to distinguish him from the senior Reynolds, young Burt was brought up in a small project house situated along a Riviera Beach canal. Although sparse, it was a sufficient dwelling shared by his parents, older sister Nancy Ann, and older adopted brother James.

An average student, Buddy pretty much minded his manners and toed the line during his preteen years. His father, a strict disciplinarian who served as chief of police,

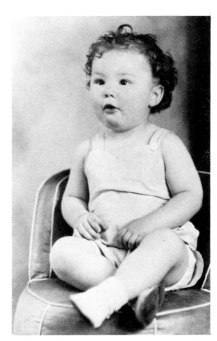

The earliest known photograph of Burton Leon Reynolds. Burt says his legs are still the same length. (1937)   11

Preschooler Buddy Reynolds shows his first girlfriend how to curtsy for the camera. (1940)

set rigid guidelines for his offspring. His youngest son didn't talk back and he didn't dispute authority. Not yet.

Buddy's best pals were primarily the sons of fishermen along the canal, and most of them were Italian. There was no need for the police chief's namesake to explain his own heritage. On one side of the family, a full-blooded Cherokee grandmother, wife of a forestry ranger, who gave birth to his father on a North Carolina reservation; on the other side of the family, grandparents and mother of pioneer WASP roots, raised in and around central Michigan. Being "the new boy in town," Burt doted on the immediate attention extended by his waterfront playmates. They assumed that he was also Italian, and Burt never corrected them.

Pretending to be Italian was Buddy Reynolds' first inkling that a person could be whatever he wanted by merely projecting characteristics of a particular kind. He was acting. He liked it.

As Burt slipped into the teen years, he also slipped into a rebellious stage—a stage that would continue, in one form or another, for fifteen years.

His transition into junior high from grammar school meant leaving the familiarity of a semiethnic neighborhood to enroll at Central Junior High School in nearby West Palm Beach, an institution whose student body was predominately comprised of wealthy society types from Palm Beach. Here Buddy Reynolds was no longer accepted at face value. The Palm Beach boys ignored him and the Palm Beach girls—and all other girls, for that matter—terrified him. Confronted with a

common teen dilemma, Burt fought back by engaging in outrageous smartass pranks and athletics. He didn't know it, but he was acting again.

The mischievous pranks came about easily —tipping over outhouses and sheds, peppering a sleeping senior citizen's tin roof with pebbles in the middle of the night, drag racing down the back roads after taking his father's car without permission, dumping manure on the porch of a neighbor, whatever.

Athletics weren't quite so easy. Too busy making a nuisance of himself and raising hell, Burt never considered sports until an alien classmate at last spoke to him. It was a challenge. Would the Riviera Beach hotshot like to take on Vernon Rollison, the fastest runner at Central Junior High?

A few mornings later, Buddy rolled up the arms of his standard white T-shirt,

Burt smiles as he flops in the snow following a 1944 Michigan blizzard. Nowadays he does anything to avoid cold weather; he vacations in warm spots such as Hawaii, Tahiti, Mexico, and Spain.

slicked back his dark hair with an extra portion of Brylcreem, and swaggered off to the appointed place. When he arrived, he was startled to find two hundred spectators on hand. Cocky and calm on the exterior, on the inside he was ready to burst. He wasn't sure if he could run at all—fast, slow, or otherwise. His only consolation was knowing that he had always been able to pour it on when running from his old man after Senior learned about another of his destructive escapades.

Determination, fear, and anger propelled him. A few seconds after the snap of "Ready, set, go!" Burt was in front of Rollison. The gallery, now doubled, was cheering the short-legged greaseball from the wrong side of the river. He was a winner. Burton Leon Reynolds would never be the same.

News of Burt's running prowess reached the athletic department. The head football coach offered the gutsy youngster an opportunity to try out for the school team. After becoming a member of the squad, Burt practiced twice as hard and twice as long as his teammates. Throughout his junior high and subsequent high school sports encounters, onlookers were amazed at his speed on the football field. He was a kid who had to run not twice as fast but, because of his short legs, three times as fast as his opponents.

All efforts were worth it. Burt had discovered the roar of the crowd. Acceptance pumped his adrenaline. He would physically exhaust himself in an attempt to be number one. He learned quickly that being top man brought about lots of fringe benefits—dates with the prettiest girls, respect

Burt at age twelve, a year before junior high school, organized sports, girls, and acute growing pains. (1948)

from the wealthy society cliques, willing students to tutor him in difficult subjects, attention from teachers who never before even knew his name.

Still rebellious and smart-alecky off the field, Burt was a consummate football hero on the gridiron. Some of the local newspaper headlines during his years as a Palm Beach High School and Florida State University amateur: "Palm Beach Delivers 13–0 Blow as Reynolds Carries 18 Times"; "Pile-Driving Reynolds Bulls Thru Middle and Goes All the Way"; "Wildcats Boast a Blasting Fullback in Buddy Reynolds"; "Buddy Reynolds Key Man Running Hard from Both Positions"; "Buddy Reynolds' Odd, Sort of Off-Balance Running Stride Carries Him 55 Yards."

After being named All-Southern ('53) and First Team All-State ('54), there seemed no doubt that Buddy "Bull" Reynolds' future would be in the sports arena. As he suited up for practice at FSU in '55, he was already being scouted by the Baltimore Colts, the Detroit Lions, and other professional teams.

Forever stubborn and defiant, Burt continued his habit of pushing the pedal beyond safe limits while driving down back roads. Returning home on Christmas Eve, he was burning up a smooth stretch of dark highway when he slammed into a flatbed truck carrying cement blocks. The

Buddy Reynolds' tweed jacket and print tie didn't qualify him for the Best Dressed list at Palm Beach High School, but he was top teen on the football field. (1952)

13

Buddy "Bull" Reynolds (on the left) always played to win. Here he fumbles the ball, but he later scored the winning touchdown to make it Palm Beach 14, Lake Worth 7. (1953)

crash ended his football hopes and nearly his life.

With shattered knees and shattered spirit, Burt became even more restless and despondent during his recuperation period. His main activities were sulking and aimless meandering. For no apparent reason, other than a desire to accumulate needed college credits, he matriculated at Palm Beach Junior College. By necessity, not choice, he checked into an English Literature class.

"I was late signing in," recalls Burt, "so I drew the last seat—front row center, right under the bifocals of Professor Watson B. Duncan III. I hated front seats, and I wasn't exactly jubilant over the prospect of English literature. Shakespeare, Chaucer, Browning. What positions did they play?"

Professor Duncan, a vibrant and enthusiastic instructor who still teaches at Palm Beach Junior College, began the semester by assigning contemporary book reading to

the class. Burt selected J.D. Salinger's popular *The Catcher in the Rye.*

"I had never read an entire book in my life," Burt admits. "In high school I wrote my book reports from the inside jacket covers. Thirty pages into *Catcher* and I was hooked. From that day on, I was never without a book—best sellers, biographies, classics, plays, poetry, pornography, anything, everything."

Doctor Duncan, who also assisted in the drama department, carefully watched the moody pupil in the front row. Contrary to Burt's own theory about his early life, the professor adamantly relates: "I vividly remember how Buddy's deep brown eyes sparkled when we studied Shakespeare or other dramatic literature. I saw unchanneled emotions and absolutely knew that he could become an actor."

It was this firm belief that led Watson Duncan to insist that Burt read for the lead role in a college presentation of *Outward Bound* that he was to direct. The exchange was brief:

"Reynolds, you're going to be in my play."

"Mr. Duncan, you're a nice man, but you're crazy."

"Readings will take place in this room tomorrow afternoon between two and three. Be here."

All night long Reynolds told himself that he was not going to read for any play.

He showed up at 2:57. After flipping to the appointed page, he mumbled two words. As he hesitated on the third, the director shouted, "Fine, you've got the part!"

For his portrayal of Tom Prior, the morose, sensitive, and unhappy alcoholic in *Outward Bound*, Burt won the 1956 Florida Drama Award and was offered a scholarship at Hyde Park Playhouse in New York.

A variety of supporting roles at Hyde Park Playhouse—including *Affairs of State* with Shepperd Strudwick, *Bus Stop* with Jocelyn Brando, *The Spa* with Turhan Bey and Gloria Vanderbilt, and *Anniversary Waltz* with Sylvia Sidney—enabled the apprentice to meet East Coast professionals who advised and encouraged him. Joanne Woodward, a playhouse visitor, was so impressed with one of his performances that she recommended him to a New York agent. This led to Burt's first Actors' Equity contract. He was paid eighty-five dollars per week for a small role in *Mr. Roberts,* starring Charlton Heston and directed by John Forsythe, at the New York City Center Theatre.

After *Mr. Roberts* closed, Burt persevered and hoped for the best. When not attending classes or doing repertory, he worked at an assortment of odd jobs—dishwasher, truck driver, bouncer at Roseland, bodyguard, dockhand. While loading freight at the docks one afternoon, a coworker mentioned a suspicious guy who had come around that morning. He was looking for someone to hurl through a glass window on a TV show.

"How much will he pay?" Burt asked.

"A hundred."

"How long will it take?"

"A few seconds—longer if you get cut or crippled."

"Give me his number."

Burt's athletic background proved to be an ideal prerequisite for stunt work. He took to it naturally and fearlessly. He made his "live" television debut flying

Football hero Reynolds escorts Homecoming Queen Mary Alice Sullivan across the gridiron during 1953 ceremonies at Palm Beach High School.

Burt mockingly toasts his high school graduation with one of his numerous football trophies. (1954)

through a glass window on a Sunday religious program.

Lots of stunt work followed. Sometimes he would even say a few words before falling off a building, diving into a water tank, rolling over the hood of an automobile, punching out a heavyweight, or being set on fire. As the months passed, he was saying more and stunting less.

By the end of 1959, after a brief interlude spent in Florida doing legitimate theater and serving as a summer counselor at Camp Keystone, Burt Reynolds was seen in strong supporting roles on several network television shows—"Playhouse 90," "M Squad," "Schlitz Playhouse of Stars," "General Electric Theatre," and others. Reviewers and critics often compared him to Marlon Brando. The comparisons irritated and distressed Burt. Perhaps he hadn't done much, but he considered himself an original.

As the Sixties approached, live TV be-

Burt's wardrobe improved somewhat in college. Here he poses in a Florida State University letter sweater for the cover of a college catalog. (1954)

came nearly a thing of the past. The major New York production companies moved west to take advantage of southern California's mild weather and technical facilities. Burt joined the migration to Hollywood. It wasn't exactly love at first sight.

A switch in agents brought about the opportunity to become a contract player at Universal Studios. Burt felt confident that his first assignment—the regular role of river pilot Ben Fraser, Darren McGavin's

NBC-TV sidekick on "Riverboat"—would establish him on the West Coast. He was mistaken.

Committed to a part where he mostly peered out a window, blew a steam whistle, and watched the boat captain play poker, new arrival Reynolds felt trapped and occupationally ignored. Adding insult to injury, he and McGavin didn't take a fancy to each other at all. Holding back for several episodes, Burt finally exploded when an assistant director reprimanded him for unconsciously changing floor marks in a rehearsal scene. He threw the assis-

Three FSU football players anticipate the '55 season. Left to right: Vic Prinzi (Burt's best buddy at FSU and still a very close friend), Lee Corso (now head football coach at the University of Indiana), Burt.

tant into a studio lake and threatened to destroy the entire "Riverboat" set if Universal didn't release him from his contract:

"They fired three contract players on the same day—Clint Eastwood, David Janssen, and me. They told Clint his Adam's apple was too big. They told David his ears were too big. They told me I had no talent."

Burt's uncontrollable temper didn't improve, and neither did his chances of employment in Tinseltown. Word traveled quickly that hiring him meant trouble. He returned home, where a Palm Beach reporter asked him, "What has been your biggest thrill so far?" He sarcastically replied, "Scoring a seventy-five-yard touchdown on the first play of the game against Jacksonville Lee in 1953." The interviewer meant show business, of course, but at the moment Burt wasn't too thrilled with show

16

Burt and brother Jim chuckle over "the good old days" during a casual afternoon visit in West Palm Beach, Florida. (1973)

business. Still, he wasn't quite ready to turn his back on a way of life that had become very important to him. He hated it. He loved it.

Within a few months, good fortune knocked at his own front door. Allied Artists announced plans to film *Angel Baby,* a story about a young-husband-and-older-wife Southern evangelist team who miraculously heal a beautiful young mute woman, in Florida. Palm Beach resident George Hamilton, a movie newcomer who had attracted quite a bit of attention in Metro-Goldwyn-Mayer's *Home from the Hill* and *Where the Boys Are,* was signed for the starring role of Reverend Paul Strand. Veteran actress Mercedes McCambridge was chosen for the part of his wife, and Broadway ingenue Salome Jens was picked to enact the healed mute, christened Angel Baby. Hamilton suggested neighbor Reynolds for the supporting role of Hoke Adams, a predatory tough who physically abuses both Reverend Strand and Angel Baby in the film.

Joan Blondell, Henry Jones, and Roger Clark rounded out a cast that wearily toiled in sticky ninety-degree temperatures in the Everglades, Coconut Grove, and Coral Gables. Burt, whose body temperature has remained several notches below normal ever since his near-fatal automobile accident, was perfectly comfortable and definitely elated to be making his big screen inauguration.

Upon release, *Angel Baby* was by and large considered to be a poor imitation of *Elmer Gantry* (a 1960 United Artists hit that won Academy Awards for Burt Lan-

caster, Shirley Jones, and Richard Brooks). Burt Reynolds' likeness was embodied in the ads ("If Angel Baby is bad enough for Satan, she's good enough for me!"), and he received sixth billing after Hamilton, McCambridge, Jens, Blondell, and Jones. His performance wasn't singled out for any

Burt's parents, Fern and Burton Reynolds, at home in Jupiter, Florida. (1978)

accolades, although *Daily Variety* did note: "There is more than adequate featured support from Henry Jones, Burt Reynolds, and Roger Clark."

Later the same year, Burt packed long johns and ski togs to keep himself warm during three cold winter months in Germany. His first foreign journey, and his second motion picture, took him to snowbound Munich, where he joined Howard Keel, Tina Louise, Warner Anderson, Earl Holliman, Carleton Young, James Dobson, and Marty Ingels in Allied Artists' *Armored Command.*

Left to right: Burt's sister, Nancy Ann Brown; mother, Fern Reynolds; niece, Nancy Lee Johnson. (1979)   17

In a World War II tale, woven around a German spy (Tina Louise) who connivingly takes refuge among a bunch of Yankee soldiers in an abandoned house while a U.S. Army colonel (Howard Keel) tries to hold a precarious ten-mile position in the Vosges Mountains, Burt captured the role of an opportunistic GI private called Skee.

Holliman, Dobson, Ingels, and Reynolds were quartered in adjoining rooms at a local hostelry and instantly hit it off in the manner of fraternity brothers. Their evening hours were spent playing hide-and-seek or nursing tall ales in neighborhood beer halls because it was the only entertainment they could afford. When producer Ron Alcorn gave everyone a one-week Christmas leave, Burt didn't have enough money to fly home. He had never been away from his folks on December twenty-fifth.

"I was terribly apprehensive about spending Christmas in a foreign land," Burt recollects. "As it turned out, it was marvelous. The German people celebrate with great gusto, endless exuberance, and tremendous feeling. I ached for my family, but it was a very warm experience I'll never forget."

Marty Ingels, now president of a prestigious celebrity brokerage firm, adds, "There was so much going on inside of us and outside of us. There were times Burt banged the table and spoke of just packing it up and going home to Florida, and other times when you just knew he was biding his time for another turn at bat. The man had a natural charisma that made the guys follow him and the ladies wait in line. It was that curious damn marriage of macho muscle and little-boy vulnerability. It was his magic then and it's his magic now."

Armored Command and *Angel Baby* were released almost simultaneously and, in some areas, were paired as a first-run double feature. Dozens of reviews included inspiring notes about Burt:

"Burt Reynolds shows bright promise for more important roles" (*Motion Picture Herald*); "Earl Holliman and Burt Reynolds in featured roles emerge as the film's real 'stars,' acting-wise" (*Hollywood Citizen-News*); "Reynolds is skillful" (*Los Angeles Times*); "Reynolds' fast-moving performance adds excitement" (*Los Angeles Examiner*); "Burt Reynolds, technically the heavy, emerges as a strong asset" (*Hollywood Reporter*); to cite just a few.

Buddy Reynolds, Palm Beach Junior College. (1956)

Burt won the 1956 Florida Drama Award for his portrayal of Tom Prior, the morose alcoholic, in a Palm Beach Junior College presentation of Outward Bound.

18

The remainder of 1961 was monetarily lean and vocationally slow for Burt. During the summer he starred in a successful production of *Picnic* at Cherry Country Playhouse in Traverse City, Michigan, and in the autumn he participated in a not-so-successful Broadway show, *Look, We've Come Through,* directed by José Quintero. The latter opened October twenty-fifth and died before Halloween.

In 1962, Hollywood and television beckoned again. Burt was offered the weekly

Burt with his Palm Beach Junior College mentor, Professor Watson B. Duncan III. (1976)

Burt was a heavyweight when he arrived at Hyde Park Playhouse. The fast pace of New York quickly trimmed him down. (1956)

role of Quint Asper, a half-breed blacksmith, on the long-running CBS-TV "Gunsmoke" series. He swiftly accepted for several reasons: he was anxious to be acknowledged in a town where he felt unwanted due to his previous emotional outbursts; he believed that it would be difficult for critics to continue comparing him to Brando if he were portraying an American Indian; being part Cherokee by birth, he was dedicated to the idea of giving some insight and nobility to the Quint Asper character; and he needed work and an income.

With the exception of more money than he had ever earned before, nothing materialized as anticipated. Throughout two seasons, silent Quint was usually seen stripped to the waist, pounding a hot horseshoe wedged in an antique anvil. Shortly before an episode was about to end, he would look up at six-foot, six-inch James Arness, star of the western series in the role of Marshal Matt Dillon, and thank him for saving mythical Dodge City from another disaster.

Disappointed that Quint Asper was given little dialogue and no depth, Burt plowed into the front office demanding more coverage and character development. Executives countered that his low fan-mail count, which they interpreted as lack of viewer interest, didn't warrant any creative adjustments.

"Fan mail! What fan mail? Who the hell's going to write to an invisible Indian! I want out!"

They let him out.

Totally disgruntled and once more feeling insecure on the West Coast, Burt approached Dick Clayton, a highly respected agent with Famous Artists Agency, who had befriended him in the past. "I know I'm crazy and headstrong," Burt cajoled, "but you're the only person who can make it happen. Get me a feature film, any feature film, anywhere in the world, at any price. If not, I'm going to call it quits and return to Florida—coach football, build barns, paint boats. I swear to you, Dick, this is my last crack at it."

Clayton, not in need of another client, but at the same time not wanting to ignore a very likable, spunky young talent, nonchalantly put out feelers while asking for a few days to think it over. Information filtered back to him that Peer J. Oppen-   19 heimer was seeking a nervy leading man for his inexpensive production of *Last Message from Saigon,* a present-day cloak-and-dagger script, to be filmed in the hot-spot capital during actual Vietnam War altercations.

Two days later, Peer J. Oppenheimer signed Burt Reynolds to star in *Last Message from Saigon* (released as *Operation C.I.A.*) and Dick Clayton signed Burt Reynolds as his own client with Famous Artists Agency. Today, two decades later, Dick represents Burt exclusively in the capacity of full-time personal manager. Their working relationship—that of two gentlemen functioning as a unit, each protecting the other across the board and down the line—is one that is admired and envied by industry cohorts.

Scheduled for two months of filming in Saigon, the *Last Message* movie company stayed less than two weeks. At the insistence of the U.S. State Department, nonmilitary Americans were evacuated from the area, forcing Oppenheimer to relocate in Bangkok and Laos.

In the role of Mark Andrews, a C.I.A.

agent sent to ferret out the cause of an undelivered message that leads to a plot to assassinate an American ambassador, Burt literally spent most of his footage on foot—running down clues across buildings, up and down stairs, around automobiles, over small boats, in and out of streets and alleys, through marketplaces, and, at the conclusion of the adventure, inside a vast air-conditioning system.

Perhaps it was luck that kept him jogging instead of shooting weapons throughout most of the film. In the few scenes requiring firearms, it was necessary to use live ammunition because blank bullets were unobtainable in Southeast Asia. Although director Christian Nyby executed extreme care in staging the shootout sequences and no injuries were suffered by anyone, there were a couple of close calls that almost canceled Mr. Reynolds' future. (In a gesture of bittersweet cooperation, there was no interference from local inhabitants during these scenes: they scattered in the belief that real battles were taking place.)

When Burt returned to the States, it

Burt's first Actors' Equity role—a sailor (with cigar) in Mr. Roberts, *starring Charlton Heston (extreme right), at the New York City Center Theatre. (1956)*

seemed that his feature film career might come to a standstill even without gunfire. Personally liking him, several producers screened *Operation C.I.A.* but collectively concluded: "Sure the guy can run, but we don't know if he can act." The roles he sought went to other formative actors of the era—Ray Danton, Michael Ansara, Doug McClure, Hugh O'Brian, Michael Landon.

Every few weeks Burt would seriously consider throwing in the towel, and even though his "Gunsmoke" savings were nearly depleted, Clayton and friends urged him to stick with it for at least two more years. He managed to keep paying the mortgage on a 180-acre Florida ranch he had purchased for his parents in 1963, but he couldn't come up with house payments in southern California. Judy Carne, his actress wife of three years and a smash hit as the "Sock-It-to-Me" girl on television's "Laugh-In," could. Burt gave her the house, agreed to a divorce, and bunked with a pal.

A sprinkling of insignificant TV roles—cowboys, Indians, romantic leads, heavies—bought him eats, Sears Roebuck clothes, and gasoline for his '55 T-Bird (now aesthetically restored and used at the ranch).

During this period, agent Clayton was called to New York on business for one of his other clients. Walking down Fifth Avenue, he unexpectedly ran into Dino de Laurentiis, a vigorous Italian producer who would soon break into American filmmaking. De Laurentiis mentioned that he was in Manhattan searching for an athletic American actor to star as an Indian in a low-budget Italian western titled *A Dollar a Head*. He had interviewed several handsome actors but doubted their ability to handle their own stunt work.

So Burt was about to play Indian again. In his depression after *Operation C.I.A.* and before *A Dollar a Head* (released as *Navajo Joe*), he had gained twenty-five pounds. He dropped the excess weight in twenty-three days.

"I went home. Mom and Dad locked me into a room at the ranch and slid three hundred calories a day under the door," he muses. "When I arrived in Rome, I was

In 1958 a New York critic wrote: "He looks like Marlon Brando without the fishmonger's gestures or mumbling."

21

willing and able—weak, but willing and able. The physical demands of the role didn't frighten me as much as my wardrobe. None of the Italians had any idea what an American Indian looked like. I wired a friend to send authentic 'Big Chief' and 'Little Chief' pictures real fast. The Italians glanced at the pictures, nodded approvingly, hacked up an old wig, and glued it on my head. I looked like Natalie Wood."

Satisfied with the wardrobe, Dino de Laurentiis suddenly decided that he didn't like the script they were about to shoot. Navajo Joe's wig, beads, and leather were put in storage while a team of writers labored over the pages. Burt sat "on hold" at Parco dei Principi during the days and consumed *molto vino* at sidewalk cafés in

As a summer counselor at Camp Keystone, Florida, Burt coached both football and drama—not the big time, but it was healthy and fun. (1959)

the evenings. In a letter home, he wrote, "I love Italy and the Italians. They are all mad. But then, so am I." (Ah, yes, rationalization from the lad who always wanted to be Italian?)

De Laurentiis refused the first rewrite. He refused the second and third rewrites. During the fourth rewrite, Burt received a cablegram advising him to return to the United States by late June if he wanted a shot at starring in a proposed ABC-TV series to be filmed in and around New York City. He was first choice if he could get there in time.

Burt pondered his predicament with Dino. The Italian producer couldn't understand how or why a television series was so important. He vetoed the fourth and

fifth rewrites. The days dwindled.

Six jittery weeks after Burt landed in Rome, De Laurentiis approved rewrite number six. The cast and crew traveled to Castile and Almería, two specks in the plains of Spain often used for foreign spur-and-saddle oaters, for a month of exteriors.

In the 112-degree heat of the Spanish desert, Burt executed every stunt he had ever learned, and invented a few new ones, for the role of Navajo Joe. Hour after hour, he performed unpredictable vengeance on a band of ruthless outlaws, with determinate emphasis on the leader who had brutally shot and scalped his squaw. He choked, stabbed, and shot bad whites (the final 116-page script called for 150 killings, thirty-six by Burt) until he got all of them.

Helplessly drained from a scene in which he single-handedly killed eleven men in one fell swoop, Burt jokingly asked director Sergio Corbucci if he might replace the next killing with a tender love scene. The flamboyant director logically proclaimed, "We have improved the American western by removing all the boring stuff. We have taken out the love scenes and all the talk, talk, talk!"

Filming was concluded on June 15, 1966. Burt went directly to Manhattan to try for his third TV series and third network. As the TWA jet flew over the Atlantic, he made a slient vow that he would stay cool and be a good boy.

"Hawk," the only prime-time television series produced on the East Coast for the '66–'67 season, centered around a short-fused Iroquois Indian detective named Lieutenant John Hawk who worked nights out of the district attorney's division. Filmed after dark on the streets of New York, each episode presented real-life situations and realistic dangers, as the no-nonsense policeman busted crime and criminals.

"The idea of a TV Indian who didn't talk gibberish or get plastered greatly appealed to me," Burt explains. "Thanks to producer Renee Valente, I didn't have to run around in moccasins and feathers. In the pilot film, they wanted me to hide knives up my sleeves, but I refused to go along with that. I reminded them that Bill Cosby had done much for the blacks on 'I Spy' [a 1965–'68 NBC-TV undercover series] by playing a black detective without racial reference. I wanted to play an American Indian in the same manner."

Burt (wearing cap) as Ben Fraser, Darren McGavin's NBC-TV "Riverboat" sidekick. "I was Dum-Dum, the Whistle Blower," remembers Reynolds. (1960)

And Mr. Reynolds' own manners were improving. He remained outspoken, uncalculated, and sometimes hard to please; but he reserved anger, hostility, and warfare for his TV character.

Miss Valente, who cast Burt as Lieutenant Hawk and has remained a steadfast advocate, unabashedly reflects, "Burt Reynolds was special. Then, as now, he had charm, vulnerability, strength, gentility, humor, compassion, and animal sex. It's a rare combination. Add a pinch of insecurity, a dash of antagonism, and a cup of 'down home,' and you have complexities that add to the versatility of the man. And if you believe, as I do, that the eyes are the mirror of our soul, look into his."

No wonder the dear fellow was beginning to mellow.

In an August interview with the Chicago *Daily News*, Burt said, "I'm happier than I've ever been in my life. I'm not prepared for a flop, but I'm not prepared for a hit either. I'm doing my own stunts. The producers go weak and sick and hide when I do things like sliding 70 feet down a rope and flipping into the water from a boat, as I did the other night, but I enjoyed the slide down that rope. It's the first time I don't feel like a chess pawn. I help direct, cast, write scripts and fight the establish-

ment. I'm falling in love with the production end of the business and realize directing is really my ultimate aim."

An absolute critical success, "Hawk" was unable to seize enough viewers to stay on the air beyond seventeen episodes. Pitted against NBC-TV's "The Dean Martin Show" and "The CBS Thursday Night Movie," the series could not be saved even by pickets or thousands of signatures on petitions to the network.

With the dismissal of "Hawk," Burt was offered a dozen different television pilots. Of the batch, he accepted $12,500 (compared to two thousand per episode for "Hawk") to star in "Lassiter," a series based on a roving reporter on assignment to a national magazine devoted to uncovering chicanery and corruption. No one bought the series. (Eighteen months later, CBS-TV aired the pilot as a single one-hour drama.)

Burt consequently opted to gamble on the large screen. Considered a product of Videoland, he wasn't dealt *la crème de la crème,* but he would never again miss a

Burt as hoodlum Hoke Adams in Angel Baby—*his first motion picture role. (1961)*

23

Burt in an Angel Baby *love scene with Salome Jens. (1961)*

rent payment. Judiciously, he would start collecting his own real estate—an abundance of it—from one end of the country to the other.

In 1967, Burt made two feature films—*Shark* (titled *Caine* and *Twist of the Knife* during production; rereleased as *Man-Eater*) and *Fade In*.

Shark, a sunken-treasure tale in which a runaway renegade (Burt) deals himself into the spoils when he learns that a scholarly diving team (Barry Sullivan and Silvia Pinal) are exploring the ocean bottom for gold bullion instead of ecological specimens, was an independent U.S.-Mexican coproduction filmed in Mexico City, Acapulco, and Vera Cruz. Supposedly set in the Sudan, the half-million-dollar effort also featured reliable Arthur Kennedy and huggable twelve-year-old Charles Berriochoa in the cast and was directed by Samuel Fuller.

Shark was difficult and dangerous to film. Underwater sequences posed a constant threat of attack from bona fide sharks. Burt was audibly reluctant to let a stunt double do any of his swimming or diving—he had yet to use a double in any of his movies—but Fuller, a director with a track record of arduous outdoor locations, insisted upon insurance for his leading man. On July twenty-fourth, a stunned crew watched in disbelief as a huge tiger shark turned without warning and tore into Alfonso Raymond, Burt's double, ripping open his left arm and most of his back. He was rushed to a nearby hospital; it took nineteen stitches to mend his wounds.

Visibly shaken and cautiously hesitant, the crew hadn't yet recovered from that very close encounter when they once more gasped in horror as a crazed white killer shark broke through safeguard netting and relentlessly mauled José Marco, Barry Sullivan's double. His vital organs mangled, Marco died shortly after the attack.

When *Shark* was released, advertisers tactlessly tried cashing in on the tragedy ("A Realistic Film Became Too Real!" "*Shark* Will Rip You Apart!"), but reviewers were not kind, and the film vanished. In 1975, during the mania for *Jaws* (Universal's stupendous shark-themed grosser of that year), it made a brief, profitable comeback when rereleased under the title of *Man-Eater*.

Fade In, a modest story about a love affair between a local cowboy (Burt) and an assistant film editor (Barbara Loden) who meet while a western movie is being shot on location in the desert, was a Paramount Pictures production filmed in Moab, Utah. Plotted against the filming of another motion picture, scenes of which appeared in both movies, *Fade In* was made concurrent with Paramount's *Blue,* starring Terence Stamp, Karl Malden, Joanna Pettet, and Ricardo Montalban. The pictures shared many common cast and crew elements and, in the long run, also shared failure.

From the beginning, Burt was unable to communicate with his leading lady, and the role of rancher Rob became a merited test of his acting abilities. "Barbara Loden was on a different frequency," he says. "I couldn't tune in, couldn't find the key to turn her on. I kept waiting for her to let loose and blow me right out of the tub, but it never happened on film."

Striving to overcome the lack of honest chemistry between Miss Loden and himself, Burt was also hampered by an avant-garde script, written by rookie Jerry Ludwig, that was perhaps too artsy and simplistic for the Sixties. Even as the cameras rolled, coproducer Judd Bernard predicted, "*Fade In* is going to be great or be a disaster. There will be no middle ground."

Aware that they might be stuck with a debit, Paramount sneak-previewed the finished product in midtown New York. The cross-culture audience repeatedly laughed out loud during serious dialogue, clearly indicating that filmgoers didn't want to sit through a simple, uncluttered romance dealing with basically ordinary people.

Many meetings and several sneak screenings later, Paramount biggies toyed with the idea of showing *Fade In* exclusively in art houses, but the plan was scrubbed and the film buried in the studio morgue. Six years later—during which time Burt unsuccessfully attempted to purchase *Fade In* privately and release it through an independent distributor—Paramount sold it to

Burt as Skee, the opportunistic GI private in Armored Command—*his second motion picture role. (1961)*

25

CBS-TV. Aired as a late-night movie on November 8, 1973, it didn't bolster any ratings, but was received better then than in 1967. (Opening to awful reviews on May 3, 1968, *Blue* was pulled from distribution and put to rest on a shelf. It remains there.)

Thanksgiving of '67 brought *Navajo Joe* to hundreds of U.S. drive-ins and neighborhood theaters. Packaged as a piece of fast-paced outlaws-and-Indians action suitable for mass America, the "spaghetti western" was greeted by critics precisely as such. Lukewarm towards the haphazard Italian production values, most reviews contained positive words regarding Burt's interpretation of the cutthroat Indian:

"The only on-key note in this film is Burt Reynolds who plays the title role" (*The Milwaukee Journal*); "Reynolds makes the most of his role" (*Daily Variety*); "Brando-esque Burt Reynolds not only has the right savage intensity for the vengeance-bound Joe, but also the athletic prowess required for his stunt work" (*Independent Film Journal*); "Reynolds is extremely convincing in the title role" (*Boxoffice*).

The forthcoming year established a lifetime motion picture pattern that Mr.

Burt in character for a Cherry Country Playhouse (Traverse City, Michigan) production of Picnic. *(1961)*

Reynolds continues today. With the exception of a respite from 1969 to 1971 for a fourth television series, the workaholic actor has starred in three feature films every twelve to fourteen months, each one shot on various location sites hither and yon. Hardly ever tiring of the gypsylike existence of a movie actor, the superstar has remained intrigued with travel. Never a clotheshorse, he finds it easy living out of a suitcase and adapting to native customs.

In 1968, Burt temporarily planted himself in the Philippines and made return visits to California and Spain.

Golden Bullet (released as *Impasse*), produced by Aubrey Schenck for United Artists, was another inexpensive action thriller designed for an active leading man. Pat Morrison (Burt), an enterprising adventurer, is enlisted to guide an older quartet of World War II veterans (Lyle Bettger, Rodolfo Acosta, Clarke Gordon, Vic Dias)

Armored Command *buddies Burt*

26 *Reynolds and Marty Ingels. (1961)*

Look, We've Come Through *opened at Manhattan's Hudson Theatre on October 25, 1961, and died before Halloween. Left to right: Clinton Kimbrough, Ralph Williams, Zack Matalon, Burt, Zohra Lampert, Collin Wilcox.*

The 1963 CBS-TV "Gunsmoke" cast: Amanda Blake, James Arness, Milburn Stone, Burt Reynolds.

in the search for a gold cache stashed on Corregidor. He meets professional tennis player Bobby Jones (Anne Francis) along the way. The search entails assorted happenings, including the kidnapping of Jones' ex-military father.

For the kidnapping sequence, twenty blocks of downtown Manila were blocked off during a weekend to make way for a rigorous chase à la Burt's earlier *Operation C.I.A.* Unable to sleep during the commotion, thousands of curious residents lined the streets before dawn to watch Burt run for his money.

"It was a good chase," notes Reynolds. "I told the guy ahead of me to knock down anything and keep going. He ran into a marketplace that wasn't blocked off. They didn't know we were shooting because the camera was far away with a zoom lens. He began knocking down old ladies as he ran and before I knew it, I was surrounded by six big Filipinos who beat the hell out of me. They left the beating in the final print."

Scripted essentially for action, *Impasse* allowed Burt only a slight hint at romance—a swift tumble in the boudoir with actress Miko Mayama (portraying the wife of one of the veterans in the film, she would later become Burt's live-in girlfriend in real life for three years) and an implied sexual gleam for Anne Francis. All this was quite anticlimactic. Pat Morrison was painted bold, brave, rough, tough, and steady.

Burt Reynolds would have to wait until his next film for wooing and winning... and, in reverse tradition, it would be the lady who would woo and win.

Levy-Gardner-Laven (producers Jules Levy, Arthur Gardner, and Arnold Laven) hand-picked lovely Angie Dickinson for the task. Cast as the sly, sweet-talking distaff member of a humorous foursome (Angie, Burt, Clint Walker, Ossie Davis) in a satirical adult western titled *Sam Whiskey,* Miss Dickinson and Burt fell "in like" with each other the moment they met.

In a sometimes clever screenplay by William Norton, Laura Breckinridge (Angie), a titled lady of means, and Sam Whiskey (Burt), a shy saddle tramp, establish an offbeat tone when Mrs. Breckinridge summons Mr. Whiskey to her Victorian hotel suite to discuss a business deal. Upon his arrival, she is hysterical be- 27

cause her parrot has just died. "You've got to bury him," implores Angie.

"Lady," deadpans Burt, "I didn't ride four hundred miles to bury your bird."

Deceased pet therefore dismissed, the beautiful temptress seduces the virgin cowboy (in a tasteful parodical lovemaking session) and hires him to retrieve a hefty haul of gold bars, which her late husband had stolen, from a sunken steamboat and return it to the U.S. Mint before the gold is missed and the family name ruined. Whiskey, agreeing to a twenty-thousand-dollar fee, recruits a wacky inventor (Walker) and an unflappable blacksmith (Davis) to assist in the comical recovery and replacement.

Silly, but engagingly puckish, *Sam Whiskey* (early working titles were *Whiskey's Renegades* and *The Renegades*) convincingly revealed that Burt Reynolds could handle cinematic comedy—indeed, handle it very well. The Whiskey characterization called for impersonations, put-ons, throw-away lines, pratfalls, and charm—all of which he delivered to the satisfaction of many critics: "Burt Reynolds is a natural comic with magnetic appeal and turns in a perfect performance" (*Philadelphia Daily News*); "*Sam Whiskey* has a kind of clumsy charm, most of it contributed by the performance of Burt Reynolds, who bears a creepy resemblance to Marlon Brando" (*The New York Times*); "Burt Reynolds combines rugged good looks with a boyish grin and hysterical incompetence that should inspire female patrons" (*Boxoffice*); "Reynolds is an affably deadpan lead" (*Los Angeles Times*); "Burt Reynolds establishes Sam Whiskey as a likable egotist right from the start" (*Films and Filming*).

Playing another heroic half-breed in his next motion picture, *100 Rifles* for 20th Century-Fox, Burt subtly incorporated the closeted wit he had displayed in *Sam Whiskey* into the personality of a half-Yaqui, half-Alabaman character called Yaqui Joe.

In a 1912 setting, colorful do-gooder Joe robs an Arizona bank in order to purchase illegal rifles for a Yaqui uprising against the Mexican government in turbulent Sonora. As he rides south to team up with

As Quint Asper, the half-breed blacksmith on "Gunsmoke," Burt spent a lot of time stripped to the waist pounding horseshoes. (1963)

an alluring Yaqui honchess (Raquel Welch), he is doggedly tracked by a U.S. deputy (Jim Brown). When the three collide, Welch switches her romantic attentions from Reynolds to Brown, persuading the lawman to join forces with them before taking Joe back to the States. In a brutal Indians-versus-soldiers showdown of gunfire, explosions, hand-to-hand conflicts, stabbings, hangings, strangulations, and dis-

Burt married English actress Judy Carne on June 28, 1963. They were divorced three years later.

memberments, a friendly enmity ensues between the half-breed and the deputy. Jim returns to Arizona alone, and Burt, in a tribute to Raquel, who is killed in combat, remains in Mexico to serve the liberated Yaqui tribe.

"As I read the script, it referred to Yaqui Joe as a half-breed," reflects Burt, "so I asked the writer where the other half was from. He didn't get it, so I decided to make the other half Alabaman—to add a dimension to my relationship with the black sheriff and leave space for a little humor. Goodness me, Yaqui Joe needed some humor—that massive sombrero, the gold necklaces, rings, pistols, knives, bandana, chaps, spurs, bandages. I looked like a decorated Christmas tree. The perfect casting for my part would have been Eli

29

Operation C.I.A., *Burt's third motion picture, was short on dialogue and long on action. (1965)*

Wallach. With Jim Brown and Raquel Welch toplining, I told the producers, 'Keep his shirt off and keep her shirt off and give me the lines.' Raquel has grit—did all of her own stunts without a whimper. And she has become more than respectable as an actress."

Even with "the lines," Burt ended up lost in the shuffle due to all the publicity generated over a solitary love scene between white Miss Welch and black Mr. Brown. The rumors that circulated were hotter than the sweltering Spanish towns of Granada, Polopos, and Almería where the movie was filmed. Mr. Reynolds, at times amused by all the foolishness, took it in stride and was not entirely overlooked when *100 Rifles* was released:

"Reynolds plays his half-breed with a full-blooded eye twitch, milking the most from obvious chuckle-bait and finding the laughs" (*Chicago Tribune*); "Of the three co-stars, Reynolds is the only one who can act" (*Cleveland Press*); "If the character of Yaqui Joe had been more carefully scripted, Burt Reynolds would have easily stolen the picture" (*Los Angeles Herald Ex-*

30

aminer); "Gutsy guy Reynolds has stardust all over him" (*Hollywood Reporter*); "Yaqui Joe is played with real style by Burt Reynolds" (Newark *Star-Ledger*).

DATE: January 1, 1969
TO: Dick Clayton, Agent
FROM: Burt Reynolds, Client
SUBJECT: New Year's Resolution
MESSAGE: The only Indian I haven't
           played is Pocahontas. I'm
           tired of shaving my
           arms—it's easy to get the
           left, but reaching the right is
           a bitch.

Burt shaved only his face and wore updated clothes for his tenth motion picture, Universal's *Skullduggery*, filmed entirely in Jamaica during the early months of 1969.

In a busy science fiction script pertaining to human rights, New Guinea resident Douglas Temple (Burt) finagles his way into a jungle expedition when anthropologist Sybil Greame (Susan Clark) lands in his territory. While she searches for old bones, he surreptitiously searches for fresh deposits of money-making phosphor. They fall upon not only bones and phosphor, but also a cheery tribe of diminutive half-animal, half-human creatures (twenty-four very short University of Djakarta students in costume) dubbed Tropis. Organizing the consenting Tropis into a highly productive work force to mine the phosphor, Temple has second thoughts as he watches Greame and her scientific colleagues monitor every Tropi movement including caged reproduc- tion habits. He flees with a pregnant Tropi (Pat Suzuki) and, after her baby is still-born, deliberately pretends he killed it; his actions bringing about an international trial to prove Tropis human rather than animal.

Not a bad bit of writing, *Skullduggery* disappointingly wound up an inconsistent blend of humor and human compassion, mostly because of faulty direction and bad editing. It didn't quite make it, and critics

A sprinkling of TV roles—cowboys, romantic leads, heavies—kept Burt professionally alive during 1965. He's in costume here for "The Dick Powell Theatre" (NBC-TV).

often used the words "corny" and "campy" in their comments. Reynolds did "bring a brash charm to the part" (*Hollywood Reporter*) and was "virile and likable in a boyish sort of way" (*Motion Picture Herald*) . . . and he looked very handsome in civilian attire.

Fairly content making feature films, and always in quest of "the right script," Burt had no intentions of returning to television as star of another series. Producer Quinn Martin dangled an exceptionally lucrative deal before him, including a twenty-six-segment guarantee, to depict ABC-TV's "Dan August," a conservative, hard-hitting detective headquartered in the small fictitious community of Santa Luisa, California.

"I was one hundred percent negative at first. Then I remembered the happy days I had spent in New York on 'Hawk,'" Burt recounts. "A full-season guarantee might

Burt in the title role of Navajo Joe—*his fourth motion picture and only Italian western. (1966)*

32

Burt with Italian actress Nicoletta Machiavelli during one of the few calm moments in Navajo Joe. *(1966)*

give me leverage. Renee Valente, bless her, had always preached leverage to me, but 'Hawk' had been axed before I could gain any. I asked Dick [Clayton] to go after 'August,' naming a ridiculous sum of money, the option to do all my own stunts, a clause to direct a specific amount of second-unit stuff, script approval, and so on and so on. You could have knocked me with an old Indian feather when Quinn agreed to almost everything. Our working relationship was like that all during 'Dan August.' He is a very classy gentleman, and I have great respect for him professionally and personally. My costars were the best—Norman [Fell], Richard [Anderson], Ned [Romero], Ena [Hartman]. Norman and his wife Karen have remained very close friends. So has Dick Anderson. I love them."

Competing against "Hawaii Five-O" (starring Jack Lord, on CBS-TV) and "McCloud" (starring Dennis Weaver, on NBC-TV)—both of them detective series—Burt made the usual strategic

rounds of TV talk shows to peddle "Dan August" to fickle spectators. As a guest on the major chat programs—hosted by Johnny Carson, Merv Griffin, Mike Douglas, Dinah Shore—he smoothly sold the Santa Luisa cop series while spinning funny, self-deprecating anecdotes about his childhood and early career. He unashamedly utilized the series and his own personality as an investment in himself, and his unexpected candor, wit, and frankness were delightfully refreshing and entertaining. Audiences positively adored him. He was rolling on a cadenced course towards leverage.

Burt starred in two television movies—*Hunters Are for Killing* (CBS-TV) and *Run, Simon, Run* (ABC-TV)—during "Dan August" hiatus periods. By the end of twenty-six segments, he felt high and sensed momentum. He wasn't certain exactly how or when, but he instinctively knew that it was time for him to change gears. It had been fourteen years since he first stepped onstage as a union actor. Not 33

34

a fast ascent, but he was ripe—it was hoped he was not overripe.

"Dan August" wasn't renewed for a second season, but it had been good to Burt—a new Mercedes (twelve feet long and twelve thousand dollars wide), a rambling Cape Cod estate in the Hollywood Hills, a new steady lady (America's beloved Dinah Shore), supplementary real estate investments in Florida and Georgia . . . and, maybe best of all, unqualified respect from his industry peers.

Not missing a beat, the ex-television star picked up his feature film activities where he had left off. Sorting through scores of scripts, he selected a lightweight black comedy about East Coast cops, United Artists' *Fuzz*, as his next project. It wasn't what he was truly seeking, but the impatient Mr. Reynolds was itching to toil, and the manuscript appeared to be a funny, affectionate tribute to all policemen.

Before reporting for location duties in New York, Burt dropped by "The Tonight Show" and served some more of his pseudoegotistical charms to late-night viewers. By chance, he caught the attention of ace British producer-director John Boorman, who was in Hollywood to transfer James Dickey's best-selling novel, *Deliverance,* from hardback to celluloid for Warner Brothers. Unfamiliar with Burt's work, the foreigner was attracted to the actor's confidence and control. A meeting was arranged.

Burt, the insatiable bookworm, had already read Dickey's novel—the story of four Atlanta suburbanites, armed only with bows and arrows, who set out on a weekend back-to-nature trek that turns into a terrifying test of individual survival when they run up against a rampaging river and depraved mountain dwellers. Raised in the South, he well understood the four leading characters—Lewis, an endurance fanatic having an intense love affair with danger; Ed, a theoretically prosperous man with unresolved yearnings and untapped strengths; Bobby, a jolly, thighslapping

ABC-TV's Lieutenant John Hawk (Burt) with "Hawk" series regular Wayne Grice. (1966)

During his reign as "Hawk," Burt surprised his mom and dad with a white Cadillac convertible. (1966)

bachelor; and Drew, a sensitive, easygoing family man. He had heard through the grapevine that the role of Lewis—good gawd, what a role!—would probably go to Marlon Brando or Burt Lancaster.

Somewhere along the line, John Boorman convinced Warners that the bulk of the 1.8-million-dollar *Deliverance* budget should be spent on special equipment, technical advisers, and transportation costs if he were to shoot the chilling adventure as he visualized it—in sequence along the Chattooga River, fifty miles of treacherous

Burt greets producer Renee Valente at a Conference of Personal Managers benefit. (1974)

white water twists and turns flowing down the southern flank of the Great Smoky Mountains, forming part of the South Carolina-Georgia border. He recommended using lesser name performers in lieu of high-priced stars for three of the four leading roles.

It followed that Burt won the coveted role of Lewis. He didn't bat an eye when told that his salary, much less than he had earned as "Dan August," would be a token fifty thousand dollars for three months' work. Jon Voight, receiving top billing and more money than Burt, was contracted to portray Ed. Talented newcomers Ned Beatty and Ronny Cox were hired to play Bobby and Drew.

Burt first undertook *Fuzz* with costars 35

Yul Brynner, Raquel Welch, Jack Weston, and Tom Skerritt. The comedy, about an extortion scheme involving several murders and follow-up pressures put on the police department to solve the crimes, slowly stumbled along—a change of directors (from Brian De Palma to Richard A. Colla), a change of cities (from New York to Boston), numerous rewrites—and Burt soon began to regret his choice. He realized that the film wasn't going to be the laugh-out-loud homage to men in blue he had envisioned. He was stuck in a cute little picture, period.

Any negative thoughts about *Fuzz* were supplanted by positive vibes regarding *Deliverance*. He counted the days until he would deposit his energies on the banks of the Chattooga.

On a danger scale of one to six, canoe enthusiasts rate the white waterfalls of the Chattooga River at five. Producer-director Boorman employed experts to train his ac-

tors to shoot the rapids, scale cliffs, and handle bows and arrows proficiently. The four principals, particularly Burt, with his stunt man experience, were better than average by the time filming began.

Using waterproof camera equipment, heavy-duty U.S. Navy rafts, ropes, pulleys, makeshift anchors, and all sorts of innovative contraptions, Boorman positioned cameras and crew along the shore, in the river, in trees, on rocks, and in the air. More than once he almost lost his men. Voight was thrown into dangerous waters many times and had two different canoes disintegrate beneath him. When he recovered from the second canoe mishap, he told a reporter, "I've lost fifteen pounds. I honestly believe this is the most physical picture ever made. I've spent so much time underwater that it seems as if we're doing a Jacques Cousteau documentary."

A prominent scene called for Burt to be catapulted over the largest of the Chat-

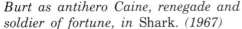
Burt as antihero Caine, renegade and soldier of fortune, in Shark. *(1967)*

tooga falls. A professional canoeist, on payroll to double for him, refused to attempt it. They sent a cloth dummy over.

"How did that look?" asked cameraman Vilmos Zsigmond.

"Like a dummy going over a waterfall," replied the disgusted Boorman.

"I'll go over," volunteered Burt.

He not only went over, grazing his head on a boulder, but nearly drowned in the undercurrents, and was dragged half-conscious a quarter of a mile downstream before staggering to the shore.

"How did that look?" he questioned faintly.

"Like a dummy going over a waterfall," sighed a relieved director.

Recalling the scene, Reynolds reminisces, "I'm not sure why I did it. It was a very unselfish film. Jon knew that he had to give me the first part of the film—he had to lay back. And I had to lay back and give him the second part of the film. He did his part, and I got hurt and lay in the bottom of the canoe for the last half-hour of the picture. It was a very giving film. No egos involved. We ate our lunches out of paper bags. Everyone always asks how we did it. We just did it, that's all. Before it was released, I had nightmares that the master print was destroyed in a fire and they made it over again using James Caan instead of me."

Opening nationwide in early August, 1972, *Deliverance* was hailed as one of the year's best films, a semiclassic, a near perfect success. Almost a decade later, it has held up as a challenge to man's thoughts about survival and his theory of masculinity, the belief that sturdy individualism can be exhibited and identity substantiated by a self-propelled primitive ordeal.

Deliverance critiques and reviews dwelled at length on the theme and technical aspects of the movie. Yet, the brief mentions of Burt's rendering of Lewis were powerful:

Burt trades a cigarette for information from child actor Charles ("Smoky-Smoky") Berriochoa in Shark. *(1967)*

"Lewis is unflinchingly portrayed by Burt Reynolds" (*Shreveport Times*); "Each of the four lead performances is exceptional, none more so than Burt Reynolds' beefy, supercilious Lewis" (*Time*); "Burt Reynolds has that old Clark Gable sardonic quality, and is superb in this outing as a machismo-ridden jock who thinks life is a game" (*Cosmopolitan*); "Burt Reynolds is a hidden iceberg that breaks out like gang-busters" (*After Dark*); "Burt Reynolds displays the proper balance of muscle and overstated courage" (*Boston Herald*).

Nominated for three Academy Awards—best director, best film editing (Tom Priestly), and best picture—*Deliverance* lost out to Bob Fosse (*Cabaret*), David Bretherton (*Cabaret*), and *The Godfather*, respectively.

After *Deliverance* finished lensing and

Burt as the star of Paramount's never-released Fade In. *(1967)*

Fade In *lovers Burt Reynolds and Barbara Loden. (1967)*

before it opened, Burt made two movies—*Everything You Always Wanted to Know About Sex* and *Shamus.*

Fuzz and *Everything You Always Wanted to Know About Sex* were released on the heels of *Deliverance.* The former received fair notices, taking in profitable returns, without an extensive publicity campaign. There were a couple of shaky moments when a pair of teen-age punks, supposedly triggered by a burning scene in *Fuzz,* killed two sleeping men in Atlanta by setting them on fire. Blaming the killings on the makers of the film, a group of concerned citizens demanded that *Fuzz* be pulled from theaters, but nothing came of their accusations. (In the scene in question, Burt is doing undercover work, posing as a skid row derelict, trying to trap crazies who have murdered a string of dozing bums by pouring gasoline over them and setting them ablaze. Executing his own fire gag when the scene was filmed—no double was used, only a back-up safety—Burt almost lost his famous face when out-of-

control flames whipped up his asbestos-lined coat sleeve, around his neck, and along the back of his head.)

Everything You Always Wanted to Know About Sex, in which Burt made a brief appearance, was director-writer-star Woody Allen's absurd sexual parody of Dr. David Reuben's 1969 best-selling book of the same title. Divided into seven goofy vignettes concerning sex—aphrodisiacs, sodomy, orgasm, transvestism, perversion, sex clinics, and ejaculation—only the title and a few inane inquiries have anything to do with Dr. Reuben's book. The United Artists fantasy finds Mr. Reynolds participating in the climactic segment, a science fiction fable featuring a reluctant sperm (Allen) on red alert to a mission control center below the waistline, where crew members (Burt and Tony Randall) valiantly struggle to create and maintain an erection. Not H.G. Wells or Jules Verne . . . and certainly a long way from Quint Asper and Yaqui Joe!

Shamus (Yiddish slang for detective) was   39

Burt as Pat Morrison, the rigorously athletic adventurer in Impasse. *(1968)*

a private eye caper with a resourceful gimmick—rather than an office, pool hustler cum private eye Shamus McCoy (Burt) transacts business out of his dingy walk-up flat in the Red Hook section of Brooklyn, where he lives with his pet cat (Morris of TV commercials fame) and sleeps on a pool table. Hired by a millionaire diamond merchant (Ron Weyand) to track down a batch of stolen gems, McCoy gets mixed up with an ex-football player (Alex Wilson) and the ex-footballer's sister (Dyan Cannon), who both turn out to be innocent pawns amidst a gang of merciless criminals dealing in the illegal sale of military hardware, not precious jewels.

Bogged down by a foggy story line, *Shamus* made up for the lack of plot with clear-cut action—leaps, slides, jumps, swings, fights, chases—and was enhanced

Burt and Miko Mayama share a brief
screen romance in Impasse. *(1968)*

by lightly delivered give-and-take dialogue between the star and his leading lady. Filmed at eighteen never-used-before location sites in Brooklyn, Manhattan, Long Island, and Westchester, the Columbia Pictures moneymaker was received comfortably, if not always enthusiastically, by main-line critics.

In the same way that "Dan August" and the talk shows had provided Burt with lev-erage, *Deliverance* provided him with credibility. The money men were beginning to think in terms of a film for Burt Reynolds instead of Burt Reynolds for a film. Fresh scripts—"scripts without Redford's, Eastwood's, or McQueen's fingerprints on them," as Burt phrases it—were the new order of the day. Among them was *McKlusky,* a modern-day action yarn about a Southern moonshiner, presented to him by Levy-

Gardner-Laven. The story was standard fare, but L-G-L sweetened the pie—if Mr. Reynolds would star in *McKlusky* (released as *White Lightning*), they would use Southern performers and shoot the entire film in the South. Burt had often considered the idea of putting movie funds into the

Beatty), Burt and director Joseph Sargent wisely made the most out of the leading character. Gator McKlusky was shaped into a powerful "good ol' boy" who is humorous, angry, tormented, and tender. It was a winning combination that audiences would applaud and admire.

Burt as Sam Whiskey—*shy, bumbling, funny. (1968)*

South—not a popular notion and deemed very risky in 1972—and was therefore persuaded to strike a deal with the same team who had produced *Sam Whiskey* four years earlier.

Working with an ordinary script, about a bootlegger (Burt) who is released from prison so that he can slyly collect state's evidence against a corrupt sheriff (Ned

But not the critics. When *White Lightning* opened, Southern critics weren't yet prepared for movies about themselves and Northern critics weren't yet prepared for movies about Southerners. None of which seemed to matter, because *White Lightning* broke attendance records everywhere— North, South, East, and West. It was the first viable signal that Southern films could make money, a boodle of money, and that Burt Reynolds was destined to become number one at the box office, in spite of the critics.

"It was the beginning of a whole series of films made in the South, about the South, and for the South," confirms Reynolds. "No one cared if the picture was ever distributed north of the Mason-Dixon line. You could make back the cost of the negative just in Little Rock, where we filmed it. Anything outside of that was gravy. We got the gravy. It was a well-done film. Joe Sargent is an excellent director. He's very good with actors."

The Man Who Loved Cat Dancing, a Metro-Goldwyn-Mayer presentation filmed in Arizona and Utah, was Burt's next film.

Burt's first full-scale love story (discounting *Fade In,* which was never shown in movie houses). Extremely well cast—English actress Sarah Miles as the abducted woman; Lee J. Cobb, Jack Warden, George Hamilton, Bo Hopkins, Jay Silverheels, and Nancy Malone in meaty supporting roles—the wintertime production was sadly tarnished by death and illness during filming.

The death occurred when Sarah Miles' twenty-six-year-old business manager, David Whiting, committed suicide by taking an overdose of drugs after having beaten the actress during a heated argument in her hotel room. Fleeing from further abuse, Miss Miles solicited aid from Burt, who courteously provided her with shelter for the night. Returning to her own lodgings

Angie Dickinson woos and wins bashful Burt in Sam Whiskey. *(1968)*

Based on Marilyn Durham's 1972 best-selling novel about a train robber who kidnaps a well-to-do runaway wife, only to fall in love with her while remaining haunted by memories of his dead Indian wife and surviving children, the 1880s western was

the next morning, she discovered Whiting's lifeless body and again summoned Burt for help.

Sketchy details of the death soon hit the wire services, and within a few hours, the small town of Gila Bend, Arizona, was 43

Tribal conspirators Burt Reynolds and
Raquel Welch in 100 Rifles. *(1968)*

swarming with hundreds of reporters and paparazzi awaiting an inquest. M-G-M lawyers hastily instructed their stars not to grant any interviews, which made it erroneously appear as if Sarah and Burt were withholding information. Frustrated and weary, they locked themselves in their hotel rooms to avoid the media.

The hearing was delayed for a month due to legal entanglements. During the carnival-like waiting period and throughout the ensuing inquest, Burt demonstrated exceptional poise and dignity. When all of the testimony was at last presented, the investigation was satisfactorily concluded.

The Man Who Loved Cat Dancing again

came to a halt when Burt was flown to Los Angeles for emergency surgery. At the beginning of filming, during a fight scene with Jack Warden, he had incurred an abdominal hernia, at which time he offhandedly taped the injury and promised medical attendants he would care for it after the movie was completed. With only three days of shooting remaining, the tape popped open when Burt's horse stumbled while galloping in four feet of snow. As he was forcibly carried into an ambulance, Burt kept repeating, "Please, I don't want to hold up production. I don't want to hold up production."

He didn't hold it up very long. Treated

Skullduggery *costars Burt Reynolds and Susan Clark. (1969)*

Burt as New Guinea resident Douglas Temple in Universal's Skullduggery *—his tenth motion picture. (1969)*

by specialist Dr. Irving Lichtenstein, renowned for having hernia patients up on their feet forty-five minutes after surgery, the leading man returned to location one week later. For his final scenes, photographed high in the mountains, he was transported to the top each day via ambulance and stretcher. The fact that he resumed work seven days after hospitalization, the exact amount of time covered by insurance, meant that no one lost wages during the delay. To Burt, invariably cognizant of the team, this was another triumph.

Burt declines to discuss in detail *Cat Dancing*, admittedly the unhappiest of all his motion pictures. He softly comments, "It was a marvelous book, and although the film wasn't as good, it had some mar-

velous moments. I played a guilty, lonely man on a mission. Making the film was a painful experience. I have no stories to tell. I'm sorry."

The Man Who Loved Cat Dancing was received reasonably well by the press and became a big hit with women patrons.

Physically and emotionally drained, Burt intended to take a four-month vacation following *Cat Dancing*, but found himself willingly sucked into coproducing and starring in four late-night television specials for NBC-TV. Just as he had been the first major star to make a film in the South, he was the first major star to try late-night TV specials. Advisers told him he was nuts. Not surprisingly, he came out smelling like a rose. The specials—"Burt Reynolds at Leavenworth," "Burt Reynolds in

47

*Burt as ABC-TV's Lieutenant "Dan
August." (1969)*

London," "Burt Reynolds in Nashville," and "Burt and the Girls"—all did OK, and the maverick movie star gained invaluable production knowledge from the experience.

In 1974, battered knees notwithstanding, thirty-eight-year-old Reynolds fulfilled a lifelong fantasy when he was paid to play football in Paramount's *The Longest Yard.* Under the direction of football aficionado Robert Aldrich, in a sardonic screenplay scripted by Tracy Keenan Wynn based on a story by producer Albert S. Ruddy, Burt slid into the role of an ex-pro quarterback as if it were a second skin.

In an almost all-male story, *The Longest Yard* places ex-footballer-turned-playboy Paul Crewe (Burt) in a swampy Southern penitentiary after he steals and wrecks a scorned woman's expensive sports car. Behind the walls of Citrus Prison, he ulti-

mately becomes the prime objective in a sadistic life-and-death football game played between the warden's (Eddie Albert's) guards and the inmate misfits.

Filmed at Georgia State Prison, a maximum-security penal institution located in Reidsville, near Savannah, the production turned out to be a fairly smooth operation thanks to the full cooperation of then governor Jimmy Carter. Nearly two thousand prisoners and state employees were used as rotating extras, and dozens of cons worked alongside Hollywood carpenters building sets. Two permanent sets constructed for the film—a forty-man barracks and a regulation-size football field—were presented to the prison as a gift of appreciation when shooting was completed.

"The TV special I did at Leavenworth gave me some insight into prison conditions," remarks Burt. "I tried to blend in

The 1969 ABC-TV "Dan August" cast: Ned Romero, Richard Anderson, Burt, Norman Fell, Ena Hartman.

at Reidsville and remain as low-key as possible. Most of the guys knew who I was. I was never frightened of being taken hostage, but the thought did cross my mind a couple of times. Jimmy Carter assured me that he would personally come in and take me out if anything happened. It was a very gracious gesture from a man in his position."

Burt hit it off solidly with director Robert Aldrich. Long accredited and admired as a forthright, up-front "man's director" (*Vera Cruz, The Flight of the Phoenix, The Dirty Dozen*), Aldrich sagaciously allowed Burt running room while he (Aldrich) still held the reins. In the brutal wrap-up football game, lasting forty-five minutes on screen and taking a month to film, the director diligently mixed up his actors and doubles with legitimate football players (Mike Henry, Pervis Atkins, Joe Kapp, Ernie Wheelwright, Sonny Sixkiller, Ray Nitschke, Jim Reynolds, and others) on both teams. The results were realistic, but not without problems. In Mr. Aldrich's own words:

"In an effort to keep them honest, it was my plan in staging the game to never let the defensive team know what the offensive team was going to do. The defense would be apprised of the yards to go, the down, and the position on the field . . . but that was all. Under these circumstances, I thought it reasonably safe that Burt would not get hurt and could do much of his 'stuff,' thereby enriching the film. This would also enable us to save his double for those shots in which there was high risk and the possibility that Burt could get hurt. Even though Burt got bounced around pretty good, this plan seemed to work very effectively for about a week, causing much surprise and admiration to everyone involved. At the beginning of the second week, it became apparent that a semipro person playing middle linebacker for the warden's team was 'keying' on Burt, that wherever Burt went—with or without the ball—this joker would try to knock his head off. After about an hour of this, I asked Burt if he would prefer that I use the double. He said no. I spoke to the middle linebacker and ordered him to play the situation and the down, not the player, and he agreed. But after another hour, this cheap-shot artist again 'headhunted' and Burt was taking a pretty good going-over. I repeated my

query to Burt about being substituted and my warning to the middle linebacker. Burt again refused to be taken out, which this time truly impressed his teammates. Two plays later, the middle linebacker was prone on the field, unconscious, with moderate injuries . . . all testimony to the affection and regard that Burt's teammates held for him. Having played a lot of football, I can't remember another understated tribute to anyone of this dimension. It says a great deal about the character of the man, the player, and presumably the actor."

When *The Longest Yard* was sneak-previewed in late July, Bernard Myerson, president of Loews Theatres, sent a telegram to Frank Yablans, then president of Paramount Pictures: "In all my years of attending previews, I have never seen such an overwhelming response from an audience as I did from *The Longest Yard*. They cheered, they stomped, they whistled, they applauded wildly."

As did most of the critics: "*The Longest Yard* presents Burt Reynolds with the opportunity to give what is easily his best performance ever and, when the movie's over, you leave with the belief that you're going to share many more laughs with this guy in the years to come" (*New Times*); "*The Longest Yard* scores a cinematic touchdown and provides Burt Reynolds with his best screen role thus far" (*Films in Review*); "Robert Aldrich has made a movie that seems incalculably and profitably wired into the box office—and our pulses as well" (*Los Angeles Herald Examiner*); "Reynolds fits this movie like a glove. He's one of the best comedic actors working in films" (*Los Angeles Free Press*); "Burt Reynolds takes his biggest step towards superstardom since *Deliverance*" (Lee Jordan, CBS Radio); "*The Longest Yard,* in spite of a couple of slightly hokey predictable moments, is almost perfect film entertainment" (*Los Angeles* magazine).

Burt remained in the South for his forthcoming venture. Filmed in Tennessee and directed by John G. Avildsen, *W.W. and the Dixie Dancekings* was a harmless, happy-go-lucky comedy-drama laid in 1957. Taking advantage of Burt's own brand of comic banter and nonconformist allure, the role of W.W. was custom-tailored for him.

W.W. (the initials stand for nothing) Bright is a reckless, fly-by-night hype artist who convinces a group of country musi-

Burt the talk show guest—candid, amusing, self-deprecating, entertaining—here with host Johnny Carson in the early Seventies.

cians (Conny Van Dyke, James Hampton, Richard Hurst, Don Williams) that he can take them from the basement of near-obscurity to the big-time stage of the Grand Ole Opry. Behaving not unlike Robin Hood, he makes Music City connections by slinging coy down-home discourses on Nashville regulars and finances the deals by gleefully robbing a thriving chain of capitalistic gasoline stations.

Others in the cast included Art Carney and Ned Beatty, as well as famed country music stars Jerry Reed, Mel Tillis, and eighty-two-year-old Furry Lewis.

"Jerry and I became, and have remained, Southern soulmates," states Burt. "Mel is very special. But we all took a back seat to Furry Lewis. That dear old man never gave a damn whether we liked him or if we didn't. He would play his guitar all day long and all night long and keep right on drinking bourbon as he played. He never

got drunk, and no hostility ever came out of him. Jerry Reed is one of the finest guitar players around, one of the absolute finest, and he really didn't know what Furry was doing. Furry would be all over his guitar, going up and down those frets, and Jerry would shake his head and moan, 'Augh! What is he doin'?' I think Jerry learned a thing or two from Furry. All of us did."

Released a year after completion, in early 1975, *W.W. and the Dixie Dancekings* was received warmly at the box office and quite favorably by a host of reviewers, bottom-lined as ninety-one minutes of pleasant, easy-to-take entertainment.

The cordial acceptance of *Dancekings* was somewhat marred by a disastrous motion picture Burt selected to do following it which was released during the same time period.

At Long Last Love, a glossily mounted   51

musical tribute to Ernst Lubitsch and Cole Porter, was Burt's first attempt at song and dance on the big screen. When the script was submitted to him, he was intrigued. "All of a sudden I'm Cary Grant, my lifelong hero, standing in an elegantly appointed room holding a champagne cocktail. Then, very cute, I burst into a romantic song and soft-shoe routine à la Fred Astaire, another idol of mine. A wonderful movie where no one sets me on fire or throws me out of a window."

Too, Burt was a fan of youthful, award-winning Peter Bogdanovich, coauthor of this Thirties musical salute, who was being universally hailed for his direction of *The Last Picture Show* and *Paper Moon*. Eager to work with Bogdanovich, Burt readily agreed when the director insisted that his live-in girlfriend, Cybill Shepherd, costar in *At Long Last Love*. He admired the gentleman's loyalty towards his lady and rea-

soned that the team of Reynolds and Shepherd would be compatible because neither had experienced any extensive musical training. He was pleased with the choice of Madeline Kahn for the role of "the other woman" and struck up a swift camaraderie with Italian actor Duilio del Prete, who was imported to complete the star quartet.

Heavy on music and skimpy on story, *At Long Last Love* called for the stellar foursome and three other leading actors —Eileen Brennan, John Hillerman, and Mildred Natwick—to perform sixteen Cole Porter numbers. The songs were used as a normal part of the action while telling an almost plotless tale about a rich American playboy (Burt) who meets a wealthy heiress (Shepherd) while his friend, a gambling Latin playboy (Del Prete), meets a flashy showgirl (Kahn) while two of their domestics (Brennan and Hillerman) romantically discover each other. Add an alert self-

Burt the talk show guest—witty, knowledgeable, opinionated, entertaining—here with hostess Dinah Shore in the late Seventies.

52

Costars Burt Reynolds and Suzanne Pleshette in the CBS-TV movie Hunters Are for Killing. *(1970)*

sufficient mother (Natwick), and they all have lots of merry musical fun as the star couples briefly change partners, return to their original mates, and continue to pursue a blissful existence.

Burt and Cybill signed up for daily vocal coaching and strenuous dance lessons two months previous to first-day photography.

Good students that they were, complications set in as soon as the cameras began to roll.

Bogdanovich elected to use a new type of sound system whereby musical playbacks were piped directly into the stars' ears via invisible flesh-colored earplugs. This required a "live" performance from them, as   53

Costars Burt Reynolds and Inger Stevens in the ABC-TV movie Run, Simon, Run. *(1970)*

they sang and danced, instead of their being backed up by an orchestra or stationary loudspeakers. The method was not only clumsy and difficult for the semimusical performers, but it was also painful and distracting. Requiring absolute silence because the songs couldn't be dubbed in later, scenes had to be done over and over again, frequently several dozen times.

Another frustrating—and humorous—incident occurred during an outdoor scene featuring Duilio and Madeline in an open convertible. Plans called for Duilio to drive up a picturesque road after the romantic couple sang an exuberant duet. A few ticks after rehearsals began on the grounds of the Huntington Library Art Gallery in San Marino, California (a wealthy suburb of Pasadena) Bogdanovich looked absolutely stymied when Duilio innocently protested, "I know not how to drive automobile. In Roma I, how you say, buy chauffeur."

Work ceased. A double was hired and new camera angles devised.

Aching ears, tired feet, and strained vocal cords often led to thin nerves and limited patience. And there were other problems: Cybill was allergic to the makeup being used; Madeline kept reporting to work with a tan even though Peter wanted her skin tone to appear fair; notes had to be passed back and forth to save voices for singing; Burt was hounded by reporters who were determined to invent a Bogdanovich-Shepherd-Reynolds love triangle, and so on.

The critics were not nice to *At Long Last Love. Daily Variety* said, "*At Long Last Love,* Peter Bogdanovich's experiment with a mostly-singing Thirties upper-class romance, is a disappointing wasting of the talents of Cole Porter, Burt Reynolds, Madeline Kahn, Eileen Brennan, John Hillerman, Mildred Natwick and

Burt as the 87th Precinct's Steve Carella in United Artists' Fuzz. *(1971)*

Bogdanovich himself. The $6,000,000-plus film is physically handsome, occasionally amusing, but generally forced in its back-fired attempt to re-create a light and airy ambiance; it just lies there, and it dies there. The 20th release may find the nostalgia road somewhat bumpy." *Time* magazine began their review with "This Cole Porter coloring book, mounted with great expense and no taste, is one of those grand catastrophes that make audiences either hoot in derisive surprise or look away in embarrassment."

On the other hand, several well-respected critics singled out Burt's efforts:

"In the end, the easy and quick-witted charm Burt Reynolds has been able to show on television comes through and he makes an attractive lead" (*Los Angeles Times*); "Debonair is not the usual adjective one would apply to Burt Reynolds, but he earns it. He sings 'Just One of Those Things' with a Sinatra confidence, even does a little tap dancing, and looks right at home in a tux and hat" (*Hollywood Reporter*); "Reynolds is no slouch who lounges back in the affluent comfort of his charisma" (*Films and Filming*).

Although it was a below-average musical, the finished product probably wasn't as bad as most reviewers implied. Irritated by Peter Bogdanovich's braggadocian remarks on television talk shows and during interviews while promoting both of his earlier box-office smashes, there were media people waiting to get even with him. *At Long Last Love* offered that opportunity. Several well-known reviewers took pleasure in berating Cybill's performance, making mention of the director's Svengali-like relationship with her, and knocking the entire project as a matter of course. Burt became a pawn in the personal attacks against Bogdanovich and finished just about where he began.

City of Angels, a screenplay written by Steve Shagan from his best-selling novel of the same title, came across Mr. Reynolds' desk in mid-1974. A cop saga set in Los Angeles, the story revolves around a brooding, disillusioned policeman bothered by his profession and his woman, a gorgeous, high-class hooker. Burt wasn't keen about playing another cop, but he was drawn to the old-fashioned morality of the main character, Lieutenant Phil Gaines, combined with the new-fashioned romatic angle. Seeking a second opinion, he took the script to director Robert Aldrich.

"One early, early morning, Burt showed up at my location trailer and handed me a script and asked if I would be interested in doing it with him," affirms Aldrich. "I read

it that night—liked the script, hated the title, realized it had some basic deficiencies, and knew we could never get away with an American lady playing the role of a high-class prostitute. When I met with Burt the next day, he concurred and from nowhere came up with, 'Why not get Catherine Deneuve?' We formed a partnership [RoBurt], bought the script, changed the title, hired a writer, paid our own way to Paris, and met with Miss Deneuve. Burt was his usual charming self. Five days later, Miss Deneuve agreed to join us in *Hustle.* Two days after that, Burt and I were in New York meeting with Frank Yablans, then president of Paramount, and set up a production-distribution deal on the picture. The movie was good for all of us, very profitable for RoBurt and Paramount. I wish I could say that most deals were as

Burt performs a near-disastrous fire stunt in Fuzz. *(1971)*

Burt as Lewis in Deliverance—*the part
that changed his career and his life.
(1971)*

*Deliverance principals—Ned Beatty,
Jon Voight, Ronny Cox, Burt
Reynolds—take aim to bury dead
mountain man Billy McKinney. (1971)*

smooth and untroubled as this one."

Hustle (briefly titled *Home Free* during production) might have been even more profitable if Lieutenant Gaines hadn't been killed off in the end. Burt was thoroughly convincing as the plagued, sensitive policeman—tribute again to the solid rapport between actor Reynolds and director Aldrich—but avid B.R. fans didn't care to see a favorite star get gunned down when they wanted him to live happily ever after with Catherine Deneuve.

Heeding that lesson in Burt's next outing, a kill-them-off ending was altered to a let-them-live finale, in 20th Century-Fox's *Lucky Lady.* Unfortunately, even with a happy ending, *Lucky Lady* sank fast and became the second of only three money-losing films in Burt Reynolds' motion picture repertoire.

A comedy-drama, *Lucky Lady* concerns the adventures of two down-on-their-luck fellows (Burt and Gene Hackman) and an enterprising young lady (Liza Minnelli) who team up to run booze between Mexico and southern California during Prohibition. Spending most of their time aboard ship, with only the spirits and each other to keep them warm, they become an in-the-chips trio and lifelong *ménage à trois.*

Though much of *Lucky Lady* was filmed in Guaymas, Cuernavaca, and Mexico City, over eighty percent of shooting was done aboard a small boat. More than fifty people, plus hundreds of tons of bulky equipment, were crammed into every nook and cranny of a sixty-three-foot cutter designed to house a crew of eight. The first day of photography, Miss Minnelli took one glance and quipped, "This is ridiculous! It's like the sight gag in the circus where all the clowns pile out of one little car."

As the weeks passed, so did humor. Over budget (thirteen million dollars versus nine million) and over schedule (twenty weeks versus sixteen), the stars and supporting players (among them Geoffrey Lewis, John Hillerman, and Robby Benson) were fed up with cramped quarters, slipping and sliding across the deck, being tossed overboard by faulty rigging, seasickness, dysentery, sunburn, and headaches caused by the stench of sweat, garbage, and nearby fish-processing plants. Unable to change course, director Stanley Donen (most famous for his "dry" musicals—*Singing in the Rain, Anchors Aweigh, Seven Brides for Seven Brothers*—shot on sound stages at Metro-Goldwyn-Mayer) theorized, "If you ever have to make a movie, don't even go near the water. Nothing stands still when you're shooting on the water."

A bubbly script on paper, *Lucky Lady* turned out to be overproduced and underwritten on film. Spectacularly eye-catching—exploding sailing vessels (seventy were used in the final sea chase), extravagant decor, stunning photography, lavish cos-

tumes, and a grandiose panoramic appearance—there was so much going on that audiences couldn't get involved with the characters. It was chalked off as a box-office bomb a few days after release.

"I didn't earn any royalty checks from *Lucky Lady,* but the picture saved me at least a hundred thousand dollars," rationalizes Burt. "After six months docked in Guaymas, I'll never, ever buy a sailing boat, yacht, houseboat, dinghy, or canoe. I always thought it would be nice to have a teakwood boat and sail around the world like Sterling Hayden and then write a book called *The Wanderer.* I've decided to stick with my ranches and horses."

Beneath the humor, Burt became noticeably worried and agitated when *At Long Last Love* and *Lucky Lady* both went down the drain within a few months of each other. He had pushed too hard and come too far to be permanently placed on the

Burt made a brief appearance with Tony Randall in Everything You Always Wanted to Know About Sex, *a 1972 erotic fantasy written and directed by Woody Allen.*

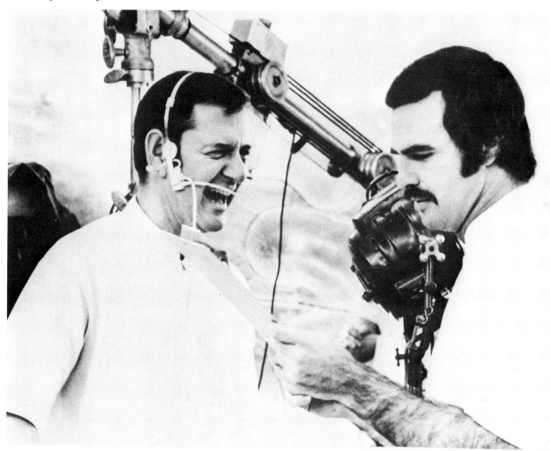

Burt as Shamus McCoy in Columbia's
Shamus. *(1973)*

Shamus *costars Burt Reynolds and
Dyan Cannon. (1973)*

minus side of a bookkeeping ledger. He advised his manager that he wanted to direct a feature-length motion picture. If the film failed, he would have only himself to blame.

No one was interested. Television films, yes. Feature films, no.

Burt "Bull" Reynolds stood steadfast.

Two familiar deal makers, producers Arthur Gardner and Jules Levy, came calling with a compromise—they would employ Burt to direct a low-budget sequel to *White Lightning,* giving him ample space to call his own shots, if he would also star in the film. Burt mulled their offer for ten seconds, shook hands, and asked them to start writing a script.

Scouting location sites in Valdosta and Savannah, Burt told a reporter, "I have this violent urge to get behind the camera. I want to direct very badly. I want to say some nice things about the South. I want to sneak up on some people. This is a director's medium, and it's up to the director how he sells the picture and puts it to-

gether."

Burt Reynolds fell into the know-how of directing as naturally as he had fallen into doing stunt work during his earlier years. While never without a comment, opinion, or instruction of his own, he exhibited the uncommon trait of listening to others around him and showed exceptional concern for his fellow actors. Shooting in Georgia, he felt at home behind the camera and in front of it.

Gator, a *White Lightning* postscript, picks up moonshiner Gator McKlusky (Burt) ten years later. Out of prison, collecting evidence for the state against a bunch of unscrupulous baddies (Jerry Reed, Dub Taylor, Burton Gilliam, Alex Hawkins, and others), he is chased by a federal agent (Jack Weston) and a posse of revenuers. As they try to catch him, he tries to catch a feminist TV newscaster (Lauren Hutton).

Almost as if he would never be given the chance to direct a second motion picture, director Reynolds went for a little bit of everything in *Gator*—a tremendous boat chase, a comical car chase, a horrendous

61

Burt as Gator McKlusky in United Artists' White Lightning. *(1973)*

Burt as The Man Who Loved Cat Dancing. *(1973)*

fire scene, an eerie psychedelic house filled with teeny-bopper prostitutes, mood-setting drug trips, ethnic humor, vicious beatings, racial statements, a gentle romance. If the outcome was somewhat bumpy and a few elements out of place, only the critics took notice. As with *White Lightning*, the public found something for almost everyone and greedily gobbled it up.

As the money rolled in and the reviewers rolled out, Burt summarized, "I'm still not sure anyone's going to want to hire me as a director, but those six weeks behind the camera working on *Gator* were the most artistically fulfilling six weeks of my life. Within the boundaries that I had, I think we were fortunate. I'm satisfied. I can promise you that I will direct more films."

In 1976, Burt was one of a half-dozen prominent stars who made an appearance in director-writer-star Mel Brooks' hilarious *Silent Movie*.

A motion picture without dialogue, *Silent Movie* pantomimes the story of a down-and-out director (Mel Brooks) who assures a financially troubled studio chief (Sid Caesar) that he can save the studio from bankruptcy if he directs a contemporary silent movie starring big-time superstars. Selling this bill of goods, the director and two cronies (Marty Feldman, Dom De Luise) set out on a zany search for Anne Bancroft, James Caan, Marcel Marceau, Liza Minnelli, Paul Newman, and Burt Reynolds. Each celebrity is tracked down by a different idiotic method; Burt, for example, is approached when the comedians crawl into his ultra-expensive mansion and sneak up on him while he's taking a shower.

In a wordless portrayal of himself, Burt is seen fleetingly—in the aforementioned

Burt falls in love with the woman he kidnaps (Sarah Miles) in The Man Who Loved Cat Dancing. *(1973)*

Guest Jonathan Winters and host Burt perform for "Burt Reynolds at Leavenworth," an NBC-TV late-night special aired October 14, 1973.

shower scene, inside the house, and outside the mansion as he is comically mowed down by a road-paving machine. He is fast and he is flawless—mockingly narcissistic, roguish, flippant, glamorous, and darling.

As a courtesy to Mr. Brooks, Burt and each of the superstars worked in *Silent Movie,* a 20th Century-Fox release, for $138 per day—union scale for a nonspeaking role in a feature-length film

at the time—and all received an individual gift of gratitude from Mel. Burt's gift was a magnificent Arabian horse.

Inhaling the pecuniary success of *Gator* and the craziness of *Silent Movie,* Burt chose his twenty-fourth motion picture with his heart rather than with his head.

During *At Long Last Love,* Peter Bogdanovich had given him a script titled *Starlight Parade* to read. A slapstick drama

*Left to right: guests Michael Caine,
Roger Moore, Edward Fox, and Ryan
O'Neal share the spotlight with host
Burt during "Burt Reynolds in
London," an NBC-TV late-night special
aired November 11, 1973.*

concerning the pioneer days of silent
filmmaking, the script needed overhauling,
but Burt was drawn to the theme. When
he confessed interest to Peter, the director
indicated that Ryan O'Neal and Tatum
O'Neal, whom he had guided so winningly
in *Paper Moon*, would play two of three
stellar roles. Burt was swayed by the prospect of working with O'Neal, O'Neal, and
Bogdanovich.

The resultant movie, released as *Nickelodeon*, was nip and tuck right from the
start. Whispers promptly circulated that
Bogdanovich and Columbia Pictures were
at odds—"having serious creative differences"—over script, budget, cast, crew, location sites, title, sets, whether or not the
period piece should be photographed in
black and white, etc.

As Peter hurdled the production

problems—some real, some in the minds of
tricky reporters—Burt found it more and
more agonizing to show up for work. With
a faultless reputation for always being
early and fully prepared, he couldn't com-
prehend why he had so little alacrity and
energy. Onlookers reckoned that he was
tired—the pressures of a plagued film plus
his gung-ho life style catching up with
him. All of which made sense until he began passing out and losing weight.

When *Nickelodeon* wrapped in Los Angeles, Burt flew home to Jupiter, Florida,
and checked into a nearby hospital. A bat-
tery of tests showed nothing wrong. He returned to his ranch and started passing out
again. He consulted another hospital. Tests
showed nothing wrong. He went back to
the ranch. Down to 146 pounds and unable
to lift anything heavier than his shaving

*An artist's conception of Burt as Paul
Crewe, captain of the fictional Citrus
Prison football squad, in Paramount's*
The Longest Yard. *(1974)*

A Robin Hood of the Fifties—Burt as
W.W. Bright in W.W. and the Dixie
Dancekings. (1975)

kit, he believed himself ready for an insane asylum or a mortuary. He began losing his eyesight for short periods of time. He tried a third hospital.

A dozen doctors later, it was determined that Burt was suffering from acute hypoglycemia, untended for so long that his adrenal glands had collapsed, thereby causing

A winning team—director Robert Aldrich and actor Burt Reynolds—at Georgia State Prison during the filming of The Longest Yard. *(1974)*

the fainting spells and sightless interludes. He resumed his livelihood two months later, but it was two years before his health was pronounced passable. Because of the long delay in discovering the disorder, he will eternally remain on a strict diet—six small high-protein meals every day, specific vegetables, limited starches, no sugars, and no alcoholic beverages.

six of his films.

"Burt and I go back twenty years," tells Needham. "After my divorce, he invited me to stay at his house. We seldom saw each other. He was either in Florida or on location somewhere. We tended to communicate on the intercom system. When we did talk, it was about both of us wanting to be directors. He got first go at it with *Gator.*

Burt Reynolds with famed blues singer Furry Lewis in W.W. and the Dixie Dancekings. *(1975)*

Photographed in color at Columbia's insistence, *Nickelodeon* was a mishmash of cutesy pratfalls and farcical high jinks tied together by way of an attorney-turned-director (Ryan), a country bumpkin who inadvertently becomes a big cowboy star (Burt), a hustle-bustle script girl (Tatum), and other show business characters (Brian Keith, Stella Stevens, John Ritter, Jane Hitchcock, and others). Burt looked rundown in most of his scenes. The B.R. luster was missing. So was the magic that had sparkled for the O'Neals and Bogdanovich in *Paper Moon.*

While convalescing at his Hollywood Hills residence, Burt caught up with stunt man Hal Needham, who had worked as second unit director or stunt coordinator on

When I scribbled a script in longhand, I asked him to read it. He did and didn't say nothin'. I let it ride. Weeks later, out of the clear blue, he says, 'Needham, where's your script? Tell you what. You wanna direct? This is the sumbitch you should direct. Take my name, go out and put it together, and I'll star in it.' So that's what I did, and that's how *Smokey and the Bandit* happened. I don't say Burt put his career on the line for me, but he took the gamble on me of doing another picture—such as *Lucky Lady* or *Nickelodeon*—that might fall on its ass."

Sharpened by three writers (James Lee Barrett, Charles Shyer, Alan Mandel), with story credit given to Hal Needham and Robert L. Levy, *Smokey and the Bandit* unfolds the tale of Bandit (Burt), a showoff truck driver who accepts eighty thousand dollars to drive from Georgia to Texas and back, an eighteen-hundred-mile round trip, to fetch and deliver four hundred cases of smuggled Coors beer. Joined by an eighteen-wheeler comrade called Snowman (Jerry Reed), the tandem takes off across America, finding lots of laughs along the route—a wistful runaway bride (Sally Field), a brainless left-at-the-altar groom (Mike Henry), a sputtering sheriff-father of the groom (Jackie Gleason, a.k.a. "Smo-

key")—and flocks of trucks, automobiles, and law-enforcement vehicles chasing each other, crashing into each other, falling over each other.

Filmed in Georgia during the fall and released nationwide in the summer, *Smokey and the Bandit* was met with run-of-the-mill reviews. It was described as "pleasant," "perky," "serviceable," "amusing," "unpretentious." Universal Pictures projected a moderately profitable run for the 4.5-million-dollar cars-and-cops comedy.

Defying predictions, *Smokey and the*

Burt as the dapper and debonair Michael Oliver Pritchard III in At Long Last Love. *(1975)*

Bandit took off like a bandit and tallied up record-breaking attendance figures. A goodly portion was repeat business—children, teens, marrieds, senior citizens—going back three, four, and more for "the Bandit" as he "put the pedal to the metal" and impishly outwitted uniformed authority. *Smokey* became a cult film—first in the Sun Belt, then in other parts of the United States. It finished as the second-highest domestic retail grosser of 1977 (beaten by *Star Wars*, the 20th Century-Fox science fiction blockbuster), racking up a staggering amount of revenue. To date, Mr. Reynolds alone has collected over five million dollars in royalties, and Mr. Needham chortles, "Reviews don't mean nothin' unless you take money to the bank. My kind of review is a wheelbarrow full of money."

Burt treated himself to a 3.8-acre Mediterranean-style villa in the affluent Holmby Hills area of Los Angeles (Hal Needham resided in the guest house until his marriage to Dani Jannsen in June 1981) and a tract of beach-front condominiums in Florida, and broke ground for a two-million-dollar dinner theater down the road from his horse ranch. An unexpected bonus was his *Smokey and the Bandit* leading lady; Sally Field and Burt Reynolds became a romantic item in real life.

The first motion picture for which Burt received a million dollars' salary—during production, before collecting a percentage of any profits—was United Artists' *Semi-Tough*. *Semi-Tough* was lensed after *Smokey and the Bandit*, though the deal for *Tough* was negotiated prior to the *Smokey* contract.

"Burt invited me to lunch," recalls Renee Valente. "I knew something was troubling him. We discussed his illness and he said he was feeling better. I asked how he was doing professionally. He looked at me almost apologetically and said, 'Renee, can you imagine they just offered me a million dollars for my next movie?' I signaled for the waiter and asked for a pencil and paper. I handed them to Burt. 'Write down how many years you've spent in the business and multiply it by fifty-two. Now, divide that into a million dollars.' He obviously wasn't a mathematician. After he

Handsome playboy Burt Reynolds and attractive heiress Cybill Shepherd in At Long Last Love. *(1975)*

Burt as Lieutenant Phil Gaines in Paramount's Hustle. *(1975)*

got the answer, he looked up surprised and said, 'I never thought about it that way.' Burt Reynolds couldn't accept the fact that he was worth that kind of money. It was very important for him to hear that he wasn't being paid for the moment, but for what it took for him to get there."

Based very loosely on Dan Jenkins' 1972 best-selling book about football, the cinematic version of *Semi-Tough* spoofed the

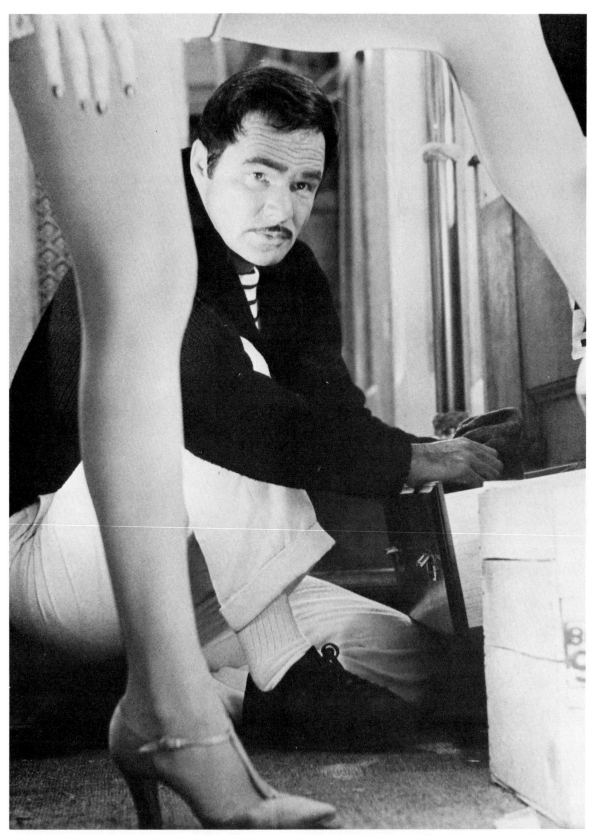

Burt is momentarily distracted by Liza Minnelli's legs in a Lucky Lady *scene. (1975)*

The cop and the call girl—lovers Burt Reynolds and Catherine Deneuve in Hustle. *(1975)*

macho image of professional athletes, focusing more on bedrooms than on locker rooms. Footballers Billy Clyde Puckett (Burt) and Shake Tiller (Kris Kristofferson) share living space with Barbara Bookman (Jill Clayburgh), the often-married daughter of the team's owner (Robert Preston). One clear day, Shake discovers inner peace through a consciousness movement called BEAT. He asks Barbara Jane to join the movement and then marry him. Ingeniously waylaid by Billy Clyde, Barbara Jane doesn't get the BEAT. Shake calls off the marriage during the wedding ceremony, and best man Billy Clyde reveals his underlying love for the bride-to-be-again.

Back in his element portraying a football player, Burt elaborated in a *Los Angeles Times* interview:

"I always wanted to play football and the experiences of *The Longest Yard* and *Semi-Tough* haven't changed my mind a bit. Before anybody knew my face, I used to sit on the bench at the Dallas Cowboy games. One night a bunch of us were going to a party after the game, and Don Meredith said to me, 'Tonight you be me.'

Well, we got to the party with all these society ladies there and I was introduced as Don Meredith, and I never had so many passes made at me in my life. But it's not just that. I guess the attraction of being an athlete is that it's measurable. If somebody tells O.J. Simpson he's no good, all he has to say is, 'I gained another 1,000 yards last year.' There's something in a good football player that makes a good actor. In football, if you have a modicum of natural ability and a great deal of desire, you can sometimes become a star. In acting, you get the same kind of chance."

Directed by Michael Ritchie and produced by David Merrick, *Semi-Tough* was filmed in Texas, Florida, and Los Angeles, at a cost of 5.7 million dollars. The film was released in November 1977. The reviews were mixed; but if only a smidgen of the critics were ecstatic about the film, nearly all had glowing remarks about Burt's handling of the Billy Clyde Puckett role. An eventual profit maker, the movie was slowed down by word-of-mouth patrons who expected a rah-rah-rah football picture—cartoonish ads showed Burt and

Kris as bare-chested football players in a huddle with three scantily clad beauties—and got less than ten percent gridiron action on the screen. Sold differently, *Semi-Tough* might have done differently.

Burt's second directorial venture was a black comedy about death, written by Jerry Belson, aptly titled *The End*. The script had bounced around town for six years and had been turned down by most of the major studios due to the risky subject matter. In 1977, it was acquired by Lawrence Gordon, an up-and-coming producer (*Hard Times, The Driver*), who sent it to Burt. As he read the script, Burt found himself

*Burt (right) with Academy Award winners Gene Hackman (*The French Connection*—1971) and Liza Minnelli (*Cabaret*—1972) in 20th Century-Fox's* Lucky Lady. *(1975)*

laughing out loud, the maudlin situations capturing his bent sense of humor. Intent on doing the film, he personally solicited United Artists and asked for financing to direct and coproduce the project. Not ebullient about the script, United Artists bowed to his track record with them—eight motion pictures, including *Gator,* which he had directed, all of which had made plenty of money. They gave him a 3.2-million-dollar budget and full creative control.

Sonny Lawson (Burt) is a middle-aged real estate salesman dying of a terminal blood disease. When told of his grave condition, he decides to hasten his demise by committing suicide and hysterically bungles

Burt directs his first full-length feature film, Gator, *for United Artists. (1976)*

Gator *lovers Lauren Hutton and Burt Reynolds. Burt inscribed a copy of this photo to Lauren, saying: "The sweater was your idea, but you were mine."* (1976)

each attempt, be it shooting himself, taking sleeping pills, hanging himself, squashing his cranium, jumping off a building, driving over a cliff, or drowning. As he relentlessly keeps trying to do himself in, he seeks out the important people in his 78 life—a dippy mistress (Sally Field), his lib-

erated ex-wife (Joanne Woodward), his plastic parents (Myrna Loy and Pat O'Brien), a best-friend lawyer (David Steinberg), his teen-age daughter (Kristy McNichol), assorted physicians (Strother Martin, Norman Fell, Carl Reiner), a very young priest (Robby Benson), and a paranoid schizophrenic pal (Dom De Luise). After all is said and done, Sonny opts to hold on to life as long as he can.

As directed by Burt, *The End* was a very funny film. It was a combination of pathos and pratfalls, with the resultant humor more slapstick than cerebral. The blend was uneven in spots, but it was real close—close enough for Burt to be extremely proud and close enough for the picture to earn substantial profits a few months after release.

The critics either loved or hated *The End*. Almost all, regardless of their opinion

Burt as Buck Greenway in Nickelodeon—*his twenty-fourth motion picture. (1976)*

Burt as Bandit in Universal's Smokey and the Bandit—*the second-highest domestic movie grosser of 1977.*

of the movie, made particular mention of the brilliant performance Burt extracted from Dom De Luise in the role of a Polish patricidal schizophrenic.

Asked about his method of directing, Burt enunciates, "Very few directors today have any grasp of the script or communication with the actors. They're mostly mechanics. You can learn how to be a require a cattle prod. They want that. I know actors who believe in that kind of direction because they're basically lazy. It takes somebody with a real gift of understanding the temperament of these people. I think I have that. If I don't have any other gift, I think I have that. Acting is such a personal thing. You act every single day for weeks on a picture. There's going

Above-the-title stars of Columbia's Nickelodeon: *Tatum O'Neal, Burt Reynolds, and Ryan O'Neal. (1976)*

mechanic, and learn the camera, if you take the time to find out. But you may never learn how to talk to an actor. You can spend twenty years in this business and never learn that every actor is different. Some you have to yell at, some you have to be sweet to, some you have to coerce, some you have to lie to, and some you have to do anything you can think of to get a performance. All of that doesn't matter. In the final analysis, the only thing that counts is getting the very best performance out of them. Very few directors understand that. Most directors feel that you go in and treat every actor the same way and you'll get a performance. That's not the way it's done. Some actors to be a day when you don't feel like acting. That may be the day on which the most emotional scene of the picture falls. Somebody has to help you. Somebody has to be there. Big Daddy has to say, 'Well, this is a terrible day for you, but this is the day we're going to get it out of you.'"

Following *The End,* Burt and Hal Needham teamed up again, this time for a Warner Brothers film about stunt men called *Hollywood Stuntman.* A sentimental testimonial to industry rough-and-tumblers, it was later released as *Hooper.* (Another film, 20th Century-Fox's *The Stunt Man,* had been registered with the Motion Picture Association of America before *Hollywood Stuntman.* Although the story lines

Smokey and the Bandit *sweethearts*
Burt Reynolds and Sally Field. (1977)

Semi-Tough stars *Kris Kristofferson,
Jill Clayburgh, and Burt Reynolds.
(1977)*

were quite different, an arbitration board ruled that *Hollywood Stuntman* would have to be changed to avoid confusion.)

Hooper was named for the star character, Sonny Hooper, "the greatest stunt man alive." His body battered and abused as he approaches forty, Sonny knows he can't

an all-time record for a feature film, to perform a series of wondrous "gags" (the term used by professionals to identify stunts) in *Hooper*—fisticuffs, gunfights, explosions, fires, leaps, high falls, a chariot race, car crashes, motorcycle spills, a runaway stagecoach, parachute jumps. A seven-

Burt as pro footballer Billy Clyde Puckett in Semi-Tough. *(1977)*

take much more and must face the reality of relinquishing his crown to a brash upstart (Jan-Michael Vincent). He quits in glory, sailing 456 feet across a river gorge in a rocket-propelled sports car. As he waits for the day of the big jump, his private life pivots around his girlfriend (Sally Field), her stunt man father (Brian Keith), and a stunt man best friend (James Best).

Director Needham and stunt coordinator Bobby Bass hired sixty-three stunt people,

minute wrap-up sequence, shot at a defunct World War II military installation in Tuscaloosa, Alabama, depicted the complete destruction of an American city. The entire facility was literally leveled by synchronized explosions, fires, falling debris, and man-made earthquakes.

Burt performed as many of his own stunts as were permitted by Warners' insurance carriers. Over the years, starting with his "Dan August" series, he had grad-

84

ually capitulated to the demands of insurance companies regarding stunts. Gratuitously, he was usually allowed to do fights, swings, slides, falls, jumps, chases, horseback riding, and some driving. Life-threatening stunts—some of the high-powered auto chases in *The Longest Yard* and *Smokey and the Bandit,* part of the speedboat getaway in *Gator,* the 257-foot free fall from a helicopter in *Hooper*—were performed by others.

"I've always been a stunt actor, not a stunt man," clarifies Burt. "I did a lot of stunts in my early acting days, partly because I wasn't a very good actor and partly because it was a good excuse to get paid

Burt, as Sonny Lawson, contemplates The End. *(1978)*

extra money. As my lines got longer, the stunts got shorter. Now they want to call in a stunt double if a scene calls for me to brush my teeth. The most dangerous stunt I ever did was a seventy-foot fall into New York Harbor—the pollution nearly killed me!"

Making light of the risks he has taken,

each other while putting *Hooper* together. Their knowledge and skill paid off. Upon release, the film was heartily saluted, even by discerning East Coast critics like Janet Maslin of *The New York Times,* Richard Corliss of *New Times,* David Denby of *New York Magazine,* and Kathleen Carroll of the New York *Daily News.* Syndicated jour-

Burt Reynolds and Sally Field in The End—*Burt's second directorial venture, again for United Artists. (1978)*

Mr. Reynolds neglected to mention the fire scene in *Fuzz,* in which he almost died of burns and smoke inhalation. In *Shamus,* he leaped from the roof of a building into a tree and the branch broke, plummeting him thirty-odd feet onto a Brooklyn sidewalk. He didn't make note of these instances because he was "cheating"—doing stunts that weren't sanctioned by the insurance companies.

Reynolds, a lover of stunts, and Needham, formerly the highest paid stunt man in filmdom, fully understood their subject matter and were completely in tune with

nalist Lou Gaul touted Burt as "giving his most attractive performance yet in the role of an ace stuntman," and Daniel Ruth of *The Tampa Tribune* referred to Hal as "the Michelangelo of mayhem, the Fellini of falls, the Sartre of stunts."

Burt's twenty-ninth motion picture role, in Paramount's *Starting Over,* was a long-overdue departure from his previous characterizations. Cast against type as a sensitive, sexually unaggressive writer caught up in the throes of divorce, he had campaigned hard for the part.

"I knew they would go after one of the

'serious' guys—De Niro, Redford, Hoffman," says Burt. "I did everything except plead—hell, I did plead—for a meeting with Alan Pakula. He gave me a listen. For two hours, I told him my life story and how it paralleled the character's life in the script. Phil Potter was a just-divorced, forty-year-old man going through a midlife crisis. I

Starting Over was set in New England, but interiors were filmed in New York while the company awaited snow for exterior scenes to be shot in Boston. The snow arrived precisely on schedule—a blizzard so crisp and cutting that the leading man had to wear high-top thermo-lined socks under his Ivy League trousers and a thermo-lined

Burt as "the greatest stunt man alive"—Hooper. (1978)

was a forty-three-year-old man holding in a lot of pain behind the jokes."

In addition to Burt, director Pakula (*The Sterile Cuckoo, Klute, All the President's Men*) assembled a ring of top-flight acting talent—Candice Bergen, as Phil Potter's wife, who suddenly wants her freedom to embark upon a songwriting career; Jill Clayburgh, as a new love interest, who only wants to get romantically involved on her own terms; Charles Durning as Potter's psychiatrist brother; Frances Sternhagen as a flaky, overcaring sister-in-law—for the romantic comedy.

vest under his custom trench coat.

In a role more chancy than any of his others, Burt was quietly funny, correctly conservative, and necessarily subdued as the vulnerable Phil Potter. Miss Clayburgh and Miss Bergen, properly portraying strong-willed individuals, were high-strung, spirited, and sassy. Both ladies were nominated for Academy Awards—the second time for Clayburgh (her first nomination was for *An Unmarried Woman* in 1978), the first time for Bergen. Publicly crediting Pakula for making her nomination possible, Candice also acknowledged Burt: "He is

87

one of the most giving actors I've ever worked with; incredibly helpful and generous."

Cinematically, *Starting Over* received a collective B-minus from reviewers. Burt's performance was viewed with suspicion. For example, Stuart Klein, a WNEW-TV commentator, asked, "Would you believe that Burt Reynolds cannot get a date? Well, in this light comedy he cannot, and surprisingly, he is convincing."

Left-handed compliments, similar to Mr. Klein's, were voiced by other critics. Acclimated to watching Burt chase women, cars, and life across the screen, they apparently could not view him objectively as a shy, passive person with little sense of self.

Mr. Reynolds rolled with the punches and kept right on moving. He next went to England for David Merrick's production of *Jack of Diamonds* (released as *Rough Cut*).

The wet English weather wasn't much better than the subzero temperatures of the East Coast. Burt hankered for the warmth of Florida or southern California (*The End*

and *Hooper* were both done on the West Coast), and within a short while his attitude matched the damp climate.

Rough Cut swelled with inner friction and tension, most of it caused by David Merrick. To Burt's chagrin, the well-known producer took director Donald Siegel off the picture and replaced him with an English director. When the new director didn't work out, production floundered until Siegel could be coaxed into returning. As the directors changed from week to week, six writers wandered in and out, rewriting and re-rewriting scenes. Larry Gelbart, the first writer hired to write the screenplay, was so disgusted with the final script that he used a pseudonym, Francis Burns, for his screen credit.

Burt, an indisputable professional, endured the daily problems and a twenty-week shooting schedule that included fifty location sites in England, Holland, and Hawaii. He was more handsome than in any of his films—impeccably attired in Savile Row clothes selected by his regular wardrobe man, Norman Salling, and

Third-time costars Burt Reynolds and Sally Field in Hooper. *(1978)*

Burt as conservative Phil Potter—a different kind of role—in Paramount's Starting Over. *(1979)*

meticulously made up by his usual makeup man, Tom Ellingwood. He looked perfect for his part.

Jack Rhodes (Burt) is a retired gentleman thief who mingles among Great Britain's upper-crust society with aplomb and style. Gillian Bromley (Lesley-Anne Down), an aristocratic beauty, tempts him into going back into business for the biggest heist of his life—thirty million dollars' worth of uncut diamonds. Unknown to Rhodes, Gillian is in league with a Scotland Yard inspector (David Niven), who is blackmailing her. When she falls in love with the thief and discloses her plight, the two of them team up to outwit the underhanded police chief. Do they or don't they succeed?

Three different endings were photographed in Hawaii. Six months later, four weeks before *Rough Cut* was released, a fourth surprise ending was filmed off the coast of Miami. Burt, Lesley-Anne, and David flew in from three corners of the earth—Georgia, Egypt, and Switzerland respectively—for the final ending, shot aboard an expensive yacht anchored at sea a few miles from Key Biscayne.

The majority of reviewers liked *Rough Cut,* making particular mention of its quaint scenery, beginning-to-end smoothness, and Golden Age quality. The public balked. Pretty people, opulent settings, quaint locations, and a surprise ending weren't enough to carry the film into gigantic profits. In the long run, it made fair money for Paramount Pictures.

Out of the turmoil, Burt formed some lasting friendships and was paid some nice—embarrassingly nice—compliments that made it all worthwhile: Director Siegel: "I do think Burt Reynolds is marvelous, extremely inventive." Costar Niven: "I would love to make every picture with Burt Reynolds—if that were possible." Writer Gelbart: "When the Indians speak of a man of substance, they say he casts a shadow. Burt has the best shadow I've met in a long time."

Back on home turf, Burt and his roomie, Hal Needham, joined forces with Universal Pictures for a *Smokey and the Bandit* sequel. Filmed in Nevada, Georgia, and Florida, *Smokey and the Bandit II* (briefly called *Smokey and the Bandit Have a Baby*

89

Burt as a troubled divorced man,
caught between ex-wife Candice Bergen
(left) and new flame Jill Clayburgh, in
Starting Over. *(1979)*

during production) dollied in on trucker
Bandit and runaway bride Frog two years
later.

Frog (Sally Field) is about to say "I do"
to bridegroom Junior (Mike Henry), when
she is called away to help Bandit (Burt)
and partner Snowman (Jerry Reed) pick up
a pregnant elephant in Miami and trans-
port it to a political convention in Dallas.
With the elephant in tow, the cross-country
travelers kidnap an Italian gynecologist
(Dom De Luise) to care for the animal, as
they keep on truckin'—always only one
step ahead of dimwitted Junior, his fuming
sheriff papa (Jackie Gleason), and various
officers of the law.

A big chunk of the twenty-million-dollar
Smokey II budget went for big stunts. One
sequence, the largest stunt scene ever assembled for a feature film, involved a hundred trucks and cars strung out across the
desert in the fashion of Custer's Last
Stand. As the "attack" took place, vehicles
chased each other, spun around, raced
backwards, split up the middle, flipped
over, and piled up. Capping off this action,
nine impressive units formed a wheel-to-
wheel bridge across a gully while a tenth
truck drove across the tops of them. It was
Needham, assisted by stunt coordinator
Richard Ziker, doing what he does best.

"I'm just a big dumb stunt man," boasts
Hal. "I never see enough crashes. Burt is a
good balance for me. When I get carried
away, he'll say, 'Couldn't we just put a
word or two of dialogue in here? Do we really need that many crashes?' I'm not very
good at listening when people say something can't be done. I've heard that ever
since I started in this business. When they

Burt as Jack Rhodes, a gentleman jewel thief, in Rough Cut. *(1980)*

A pair of beauties—Burt Reynolds and Lesley-Anne Down in Rough Cut. *(1980)*

tell me something is impossible, an alarm goes off inside. I'm determined to prove them wrong."

Those last four sentences could have easily been spoken by Mr. Reynolds. It is the key to the lasting friendship between the two men.

Another stunt, filmed at Atlanta's Lakewood Fairgrounds (property which Reynolds, Needham, and producer Albert S. Ruddy have since leased to house a motion picture studio), included the total collapse of a half-mile-long roller coaster. On cue, set off by explosives equal to twenty sticks of dynamite, the sixty-five-year-old amusement park ride toppled to the ground like a row of dominoes.

A portion of the Florida footage was filmed at Burt's own ranch in Jupiter. For one scene, depicting a bowl event, 650 local residents were hired as extras at thirty-five dollars per day. It was Burt's means of giving recognition to his neighbors and putting his home town in the spotlight.

Smokey II was augmented by a fine musical sound track prepared by music supervisor Snuff Garrett. The track included

appropriate country hits sung by Brenda Lee, Roy Rogers, The Statler Brothers, Mel Tillis, Tanya Tucker, and Don Williams, as well as a catchy tune, warbled by Burt, titled "Let's Do Something Cheap and Superficial." Lee, Tillis, Williams, and The Statler Brothers all had small roles in the movie, as did football stars Terry Bradshaw, "Mean Joe" Green, and Joe Klecko. Pat McCormick and Paul Williams again played father and son.

Opening nationwide on August 15, 1980, *Smokey and the Bandit II* earned a record-breaking eleven million dollars over that first weekend period. Ultimately, it didn't do as well as the first *Smokey,* but Universal did fine, and everyone came out in the black.

Resolving "not to drive a car over thirty-five miles an hour" in his next outing, Burt signed with Paramount to do a modern romantic comedy called *Paternity.* Rehearsals were to begin in a month, so he ordered tickets for a leisurely three-week vacation cruise from California to Florida via the Panama Canal.

Producers Albert S. Ruddy and Raymond

Bandit rides again—Burt in Universal's Smokey and the Bandit II. *(1980)*

93

Bandit and Frog—Burt Reynolds and
Sally Field—in Smokey and the Bandit
II. *(1980)*

Burt Reynolds as cross-country racer
J.J. McClure in The Cannonball Run.
(1981)

Chow threw him a pitch. If he would forgo his voyage, they would pay him five million dollars—the highest on-the-line salary ever paid to any motion picture star —plus a sizable percentage of the profits, for twenty days' work in *The Cannonball Run,* a car-race comedy to be directed by Hal Needham.

"It was immoral to offer anyone that kind of money," remarks Burt. "It would have been even more immoral to turn it down." (At his request, one million dollars of the money was donated to the Florida State University School of Theatre.)

Based on an illegal race that has actually been run five times from the East

A popular duo—Farrah Fawcett and Burt Reynolds in The Cannonball Run. *(1981)*

Coast to the West Coast, *The Cannonball Run* has absolutely no rules or regulations. Any type of road vehicle is eligible and any route may be taken. Simply, the team that makes it from a certain point in the east to a finish line in California in the least amount of time is the winner.

In the film treatment, Burt is a businessman who teams up with Dom De Luise, a madcap mechanic, to drive an ambulance. Farrah Fawcett is their make-believe patient, and Jack Elam is her stretcher-side physician. A driven quartet, they are only four of twenty-four principals in the film. Others who take part in the shenanigans include Roger Moore, Dean

Burt as Buddy Evans, a Manhattan businessman in search of a surrogate mother, in Paternity. *(1981)*

Paternity players Burt Reynolds and Beverly D'Angelo. (1981)

Martin, Sammy Davis, Jr., Adrienne Barbeau, Terry Bradshaw, Bert Convy, Jamie Farr, Peter Fonda, Bianca Jagger, Molly Picon, and Mel Tillis.

Part of the film was made in Nevada and southern California, but most of *The Cannonball Run* was done in Georgia. Asked why he went back to Georgia again, Mr. Needham replied, "It's Burt's 'good luck state,' and they treat us so well."

Two low-budget 1976 pictures, *The Gumball Rally* and *Cannonball,* both dealt with the same bootleg cross-country race. The actual event is technically known as "The Cannonball Sea-to-Shining-Sea Memorial Trophy Dash." The event's originator, Brock Yates, wrote the screenplay for the Reynolds starrer and had nothing to do with the other two films. *The Cannonball Sea-to Shining-Sea Memorial Trophy Dash* was the working title of the movie until the Motion Picture Association of America gave 20th Century-Fox clearance to use *The Cannonball Run.*

Not as stunt-defined as previous Reynolds-Needham enterprises, *The Cannonball Run* emphasized comedy, the stunts serving the humor rather than being the source of it. Purposely slanted towards an international market due to the participation of Hong Kong–based Raymond Chow (well known for launching the films of martial arts hero Bruce Lee), it solidly enamored Burt as a box-office favorite in the Orient. A recognized superstar in Europe since 1974, it was not until after this free-for-all comedy that he captured an Eastern Hemisphere following. *The Cannonball Run* turned out to be the best vacation Burt Reynolds never took.

Leaving filmmates Needham and De Luise behind—he had made four movies with each of them, two with both of them together—Burt took on *Paternity,* an up-to-date comedy taking place in New York.

Solvent and successful as he celebrates his forty-fourth birthday, playboy Buddy Evans (Burt) has everything in life he has ever wanted—except a child. Buddy adores children, but he's not the marrying kind,

Burt as Sharky in Sharky's Machine—*his thirty-fourth motion picture. (1981)*

and none of the women he dates is suitable for parenthood. Aware that time is running short, he searches for a surrogate mother to bear his child. Maggie Harden (Beverly D'Angelo), a music student in need of money, agrees to have his baby for a fee of fifty thousand dollars. The arrangement becomes complicated when Maggie falls in love with Evans.

Written by motion picture newcomer Charlie Peters, *Paternity* was brought to

successful man who yearns for an offspring, yet is saddled with too many career responsibilities to look after a youngster properly—is very much akin to Burt's own personal quandary. Director Steinberg instructed actor Reynolds to play Buddy Evans primarily as himself.

"The Burt Reynolds that I love and admire more than any other Burt Reynolds is the one he displays when he hosts 'The Tonight Show,'" says Steinberg. "For *Pater-*

Rachel Ward, Burt's love interest in Sharky's Machine. *(1981)*

Burt's attention by comedian David Steinberg, whom Burt had used as an actor in *The End*. Burt was promptly smitten with the script and asked Steinberg if he would direct it. He realized that David had never directed a feature, but he sensed that the multitalented comedian was the person to best kindle the ambiance of the material.

The essence of *Paternity*—an inordinately

nity, I told him to be that person, the person he has never been in any film."

It was a smashing formula—Charlie Peters' crackling words delivered by a character behaving in a manner that Burt's preconditioned audiences would perceive as nonintrusive. With the exception of a costly four-month shutdown brought about by an actors' strike a week after photography began, the film was Burt's long-awaited "right script" under the right conditions.

On March 2, 1981, Burt commenced work, as star and director, on a slick actioner called *Sharky's Machine*.

Adapted from William Diehl's 1978 best-selling novel of the same title, *Sharky's* *Machine* covers and uncovers a lot of territory—drugs, prostitution, political corruption, Mafia activities—as it unspools the story of an Atlanta police detective named Sharky (Burt) who is trying to solve the attempted murder of a sumptuous high-priced call girl (Rachel Ward). As he nar-

An artist's vision of Burt as Sheriff Ed Earl Dodd in Universal's The Best Little Whorehouse in Texas. *(1981)*

Dolly Parton, Burt's musical costar in The Best Little Whorehouse in Texas. *(1981)*

rows down clues, he discovers that the girl is linked to an ambitious politician (Earl Holliman) and a devious underworld crime czar (Vittorio Gassman).

Prior to publication, Diehl's book had found its way to Georgia booster Reynolds when Sidney Sheldon, the renowned author, told him about it at a party. After reading only a few pages, Burt went shopping for the motion picture rights. Newly formed Orion Pictures obliged him, keeping the property warm until he fulfilled his other commitments.

Locationed entirely in Atlanta, *Sharky's Machine* wrapped in June and is scheduled for national release in early 1982.

As *The Films of Burt Reynolds* goes to press, Burt is concentrating on singing and dancing lessons in preparation for his upcoming role of Sheriff Ed Earl Dodd in Universal's movie version of the hit Broadway show *The Best Little Whorehouse in Texas.* He and costar Dolly Parton—a team anticipated to be box-office dynamite—are due to start filming the foot-stompin' musical in late 1981. It will be Mr. Reynolds' thirty-fifth motion picture.

Free of Marlon Brando comparisons many movies ago, Burt's current cinematic image—that of a "good ol' boy"—is another case of mistaken identity. Portraying a Southerner in only six of nineteen motion pictures between 1973 and 1980, he very cleverly slithered across the screen larger than life, making everything look easy and spontaneous. It wasn't. But be that as it may, audiences enviously cheered him on as some critics jealously put him down. Today, those same critics continue to treat him with slight regard, insinuating that his phenomenal success is that of a gambler who has hit the number by chance. It is an image—call it a curse—that Burt is hungry, perhaps obsessed, to rectify.

A meager 8.5 percent of Burt Reynolds' total motion picture output—*Lucky Lady, At Long Last Love,* and *Nickelodeon*—has lost money. Without exception, all of his films that have been run on network television have beaten out the competition. It is an incredible achievement by a man who is a definite original, a resilient craftsman who takes his job seriously while managing to have fun at it.

"When it's no longer fun," pledges Burt, "I'll do like Cary Grant—turn my back and walk away."

THE FILMS

NOTE: Motion picture release dates sometimes differ from dates photographs were taken.

ANGEL BABY

"George Hamilton beat me up in this film.
Does that tell you something?"

—B.R.

CREDITS

(Allied Artists—1961)
Producer, Thomas F. Woods; Associate Producer, Francis Schwartz; Director, Paul Wendkos; Screenwriters, Orin Borsten, Paul Mason, Samuel Roeca from the novel, *Jenny Angel,* by Elsie Oaks Barber; Cinematographers, Haskell Wexler, Jack Marta; Editor, Betty J. Lane; Art Director, Val Tamelin; Set Designer, Sid Clifford; Music, Wayne Shanklin; Assistant Director, Leonard Kazman; Running Time, 97 minutes

The ads proclaimed: "If she's bad enough for Satan, she's good enough for me!" Salome Jens as Angel Baby and Burt Reynolds as Hoke Adams.

Dudley Remus, Barbara Biggart, and Burt attend an Angel Baby *revival meeting. Mr. Remus is currently the production manager at the Burt Reynolds Dinner Theatre in Jupiter, Florida.*

CAST

Paul Strand, George Hamilton; *Sarah Strand*, Mercedes McCambridge; *Angel Baby*, Salome Jens; *Mollie Hays*, Joan Blondell; *Ben Hays*, Henry Jones; *Hoke Adams*, Burt Reynolds; *Sam Wilcox*, Roger Clark; *Otis Finch*, Dudley Remus; *Ma Brooks*, Victoria Adams; *Big Cripple*, Harry Swoger; *Farm Girl*, Barbara Biggart; *Little Boy*, Davy Biladeau

PICK OF THE CRITICS

James Powers—*Hollywood Reporter*—May 8, 1961

There is a considerable vigor and a freshness that comes from enthusiasm and intelligence in *Angel Baby*, enough of both to compensate for some rough edges and loose ends. It is a departure of sorts for Paul Wendkos, who has already demonstrated an ability with more conventional film matter. The Allied Artists release bears a strong similarity to *Elmer Gantry*, being concerned with the seamier aspects of evangelism. It will have the same appeal the earlier picture did. Thomas F. Woods produced *Angel Baby* on his own, then made a deal with Allied.

George Hamilton plays a young evangelist who is married to an older woman, Mercedes McCambridge, who has moulded him in the role of an honest preacher. When his prayers restore the speech of the young girl, Salome Jens, Hamilton's life is complicated by his growing affection for the girl. Miss Jens, who plays the title role, becomes an evangelist on her own, manipu- 105

George Hamilton socks it to Burt.

Hoke rips off the sleeve of Angel Baby's *robe when she ignores his advances.*

lated by unscrupulous promoters for their gain. The climax is the reaction of the faithful when they discover they have been duped. It resembles *Gantry* in its vortex of emotion and physical destruction.

The screenplay by Orin Borsten, Samuel Roeca and Paul Mason, from a novel, *Jenny Angel,* by Elsie Oaks Barber, has a tendency to ramble. There is also a habit of some of the leading characters to speak what is apparently intended to be country speech but sounds uncomfortably like a minstrel show. It is distracting. Nevertheless, Wendkos has imparted to the film a vividness and an earthy reality that make up for technical deficiencies.

Hamilton gives the best performance since his film bow, achieving an intensity and energy he has seemed to lack in some of his roles between then and now. Miss McCambridge gives her usual solid portrayal, and Joan Blondell and Henry Jones contribute comic relief that is intelligently conceived and projected. Miss Jens, a great success on the New York stage, gives promise.

Photography, by Haskell Wexler and Jack Marta, is exceptionally good. Wayne Shanklin's music, including several gospel songs, is another value.

ARMORED COMMAND

"It was the one picture of his in which Howard Keel didn't sing. That was a terrible mistake."

—B.R.

CREDITS
(Allied Artists—1961)
Producer/Screenwriter, Ron W. Alcorn; Director, Byron Haskin; Cinematographer, Ernest Haller; Editor, Walter Hannemann; Art Director, Hans Berthel; Music, Bert Grund; Assistant Director, Frank Guthke; Special Effects, Augie Lohman; Technical Adviser, Lieutenant Colonel Thomas A. Ryan; Running Time, 98 ½ minutes

Burt, as show-off Skee, flexes his muscles for the troops.

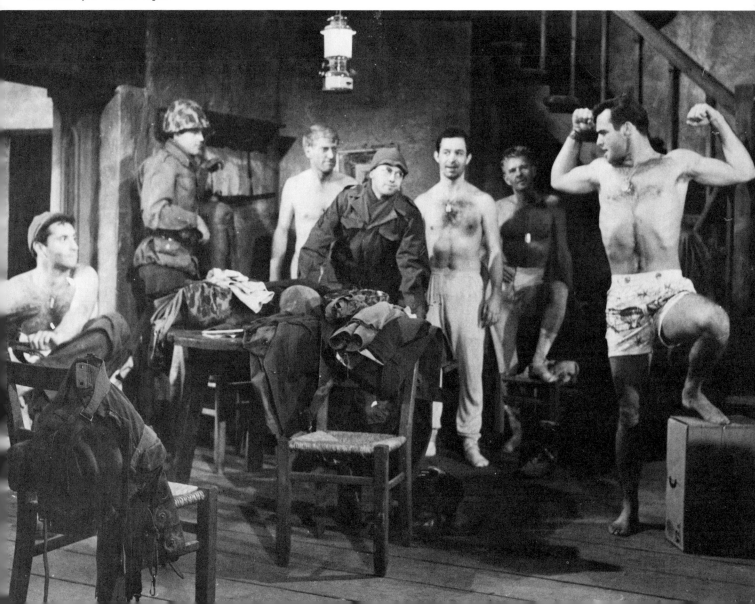

Left to right: Burt Reynolds, Tina Louise, Marty Ingels, James Dobson, Clem Harvey.

CAST

Colonel Devlin, Howard Keel; *Alexandra Bastegar,* Tina Louise; *Lieutenant Colonel Wilson,* Warner Anderson; *Mike,* Earl Holliman; *Captain Macklin,* Carleton Young; *Skee,* Burt Reynolds; *Arab,* James Dobson; *Pinhead,* Marty Ingels; *Tex,* Clem Harvey; *Jean Robert (Baker),* Maurice Marsac; *The Major,* Thomas A. Ryan; *Little General,* Peter Capell; *Captain Swain,* Charles Nolte

PICK OF THE CRITICS

Jonah M. Ruddy—*Hollywood Diary*—August 15, 1961

Armored Command, filmed entirely in Germany with the full cooperation of the U.S. Army and with the approval of the Department of Defense, is an action-packed wartime story of the Armored Command during the winter of 1944.

Without Tina Louise, a magnificent female, with or without her overcoat, this would have been a pedestrian yarn of men and tanks in battle. With Tina, portraying a German espionage agent, the story has color and the substantial element of sex and conflict.

Byron Haskin gets all he can with his able direction out of Ron Alcorn's screenplay which, unfortunately, lacks development of character and often relies on cliché situation and dialogue to complement sequences of hard action.

The opening of *Armored Command* is tense and taut as Tina Louise is "planted" in the snow-covered scouting area of the tank corps. She is picked up by Earl Holliman, a tough sergeant, and taken back into the village, where, surprisingly enough, she is installed in the upstairs bedroom of a house commandeered by the platoon.

Tina is suffering from a flesh wound in the shoulder. Instead of calling the medics, Holliman does a creditable job of first aid and, at the same time, gets a good dekko of the luscious peasant who is really a Nazi spy.

This is the time of the last drive of the Nazi Panzer Divisions and Tina's boss wants to know the disposition of the American armor at a specific time. Tina has her contact in the village and gets the information out very cunningly. Sergeant Holliman has fallen for her, but good soldier that he is, he maintains remarkable self-control.

This ain't the case with Burt Reynolds, the incorrigible of the outfit. Pretending to have twisted his ankle on a night-scouting party, he stays behind in the house when the rest leave again on a night raid for prisoners—a very realistic and exciting episode. Taking a bottle with him, he visits our alluring spy, and after a couple of slugs of cognac, he has his will with her.

Next day, Holliman, noticing the empty bottle beside her bed, the bruises on her face and the scratches on Reynolds' cheek, deduces fast. There follows one helluva fight, in the house and out onto the snow-covered ground, until the colonel, Howard Keel, who's always prowling around in his jeep, stops them.

Then the tank battle is on. The Panzers attack in force, but are held at the key points, then outflanked at the breakthrough.

Burt Reynolds is killed while holding the road with a heavy machine gun. Sergeant Holliman shoots Tina as she is sniping from the window of the bedroom, and the Armored Command rolls over the retreating Panzers.

As the tank commander, Howard Keel is ruggedly forceful. Tina Louise handles a difficult portrayal very well. Warner Anderson, Earl Holliman, Burt Reynolds, James Dobson, Marty Ingels and Clem Harvey do well with their roles, creating memorable characters and identifiable types.

Producer Ron W. Alcorn, who wrote the script as well, has a good exploitation film in *Armored Command*, realistically photographed in black and white by veteran cinematographer, Ernest Haller.

Burt in Armored Command.

Skee prepares for lovemaking with spy Alexandra Bastegar.

James Dobson looks on as Burt and
Earl Holliman slug it out.

110

OPERATION C.I.A.

"The lobby poster said: 'The Hottest Spot on Earth!' It was. The movie wasn't."
—B.R.

CREDITS

(Allied Artists—1965)
Producer, Peer J. Oppenheimer; Associate Producer Leonard "Buzz" Blair; Director, Christian Nyby; Screenwriters, Bill S. Ballinger, Peer J. Oppenheimer from a story by Peer J. Oppenheimer; Cinematographer, Richard Moore; Editors, Joseph Gluck, George Watters; Music, Paul Dunlap; Assistant Director, Santa Pestonji; Running Time, 90 minutes

Burt as government agent Mark Andrews in an Operation C.I.A. *scene with John Hoyt and Danielle Aubry.*

CAST

Mark Andrews, Burt Reynolds; *Kim-Chinh,* Kieu Chinh; *Denise Dalbert,* Danielle Aubry; *Wells,* John Hoyt; *Withers,* Cyril Collick; *Professor Yen,* Victor Diaz; *Frank Decker,* William Catching; *Stacey,* Marsh Thompson; *1st American Officer,* John Laughinghouse; *2nd American Officer,* Frank Estes; *Terrorist,* Chaiporn; *Porter,* Santi; *Ming-Tah,* Juanita; *Embassy Marine,* Michael Schwiner; *Man in Bed,* Robert Gulbranson; *Girl in Bed,* Janet Russell

Burt and Danielle Aubry talk it over in a small Saigon hotel room.

Reynolds bashes a bad guy over the head with a break-away chair.

Burt Reynolds and Kieu Chinh try to make fast time in a slow boat.

Oppenheimer and Bill S. Ballinger, as based on an original Oppenheimer effort, involves Central Intelligence Agency man, Burt Reynolds, and the difficult, demanding task of ascertaining details in a plot that would have the U.S. ambassador in Saigon assassinated. Christian Nyby has directed forcefully, conveying the immediacy and impact of the international intrigue now very much part and parcel of the Vietnam scene. For good measure, Oppenheimer took his cast to Saigon for authenticity, the footage elevating the picture well above similarly toned dramas. Danielle Aubry has some moments as a femme fatale and Victor Diaz is properly suave as one of the villains. Some greater scripting stress on character development, per se, could have rated this as significant entertainment.

NAVAJO JOE

*"The hero's greatest love was money.
Maybe I haven't come so far after all."*
— *B.R.*

CREDITS
(United Artists—1967)
Executive Producer, Dino de Laurentiis; Producers, Ermanno Donati, Luigi Carpentieri; Director, Sergio Corbucci; Screenwriters, Dean Craig, Fernando Di Leo from a story by Ugo Pirro; Cinematographer, Silvano Ippoliti; Editor (no credit); Art Director, Aurelia Grugnola; Music, Ennio Morricone; Assistant Director, Deodato Ruggero; Running Time, 89 minutes

Burt as the title star of Navajo Joe.

Navajo Joe *exteriors were filmed in Spain.*

CAST

Joe, Burt Reynolds; *Duncan,* Aldo Sanbrell; *Estella,* Nicoletta Machiavelli; *Maria,* Tanya Lopert; *Rattigan,* Fernando Rey; *Barbara,* Franca Polesello; *Geraldine,* Lucia Modugno; *Lynne,* Pierre Cressoy; *Chuck,* Nino Imparato; *Sancho,* Alvaro De Luna; *Honor,* Valeria Sabel; *Clay,* Mario Lanfranchi; *Jeffrey,* Lucio Rosato; *Monkey,* Simon Arriaga; *El Gordo,* Cris Huerta; *El Cojo,* Angel Ortiz; *Reagan,* Fianni Di Stolfo; *Blackwood,* Angel Alvarez; *Bandit,* Rafael Albaicin

Bloodshed and retribution in the old western tradition are the components of this outdoor action drama, an Italian-Spanish co-production shot in Technicolor. The protagonist is an Indian with nerves of steel and the killing instinct of a panther, played by Burt Reynolds. The story is filled with standard elements and as westerns go it should be well received in the market.

An outlaw band, headed by a sullen leader, Aldo Sanbrell, sweeps like a desolating plague across the countryside, burning, killing, and looting. Reynolds nurtures a cold hatred of Sanbrell and his henchmen. One by one he cuts down the ranks of their numbers.

The screenplay by Dean Craig and Fernando Di Leo gets underway in earnest when one of the townspeople, a doctor who hides under a cloak of respectability,

Executive producer Dino de Laurentiis wanted an actor who could do his own stunts—and he got him!

Navajo Joe is tied ...

116

makes an alliance with the bandit chieftain to hijack a bank train and share in the rich haul of currency.

As the story proceeds the Indian saves the train from the outlaws and guides it safely into the hands of the townspeople. He receives little thanks as they simply do not respect or trust an Indian.

For those who want to draw contemporary social parallels, there is material at hand. Sergio Corbucci's direction has kept the action moving at a steady clip. A slight romantic thread in the story centers around Reynolds and Nicoletta Machiavelli, a pretty Indian.

As the bandits are about to converge on the virtually defenseless town Reynolds is prevailed upon to act as a protector. He wages a one-man war against the outlaws. It leads to the inevitable climax in which Reynolds meets his enemy face to face.

. . . and strung upside down before . . .

. . . getting his revenge.

117

SHARK

*"Sammy Fuller gets the job done. The plaudits he received after **The Big Red One** (1980) were long overdue."*

—B.R.

CREDITS
(Excelsior—1970)

Producers, Skip Steloff, Marc Cooper; Director, Samuel Fuller; Screenwriters, Samuel Fuller, John Kingsbridge; Cinematographer, Raul Martinez Solares; Editor, Carlos Savage; Art Director, Manuel Fontanals; Music, Carlos Moroyoqui; Assistant Director, Rafael Portillo; Running Time, 92 minutes

Burt, as Caine, confronts an early-morning intruder.

CAST

Caine, Burt Reynolds; *Mallare,* Barry Sullivan; *Doc,* Arthur Kennedy; *Anna,* Silvia Pinal; *Barok,* Enrique Lucero; *Smoky-Smoky,* Charles Berriochoa; *Latalla,* Manuel Alvarado; *Asha,* Emilia Suart

PICK OF THE CRITICS

Roger Greenspun—*The New York Times*—June 16, 1970

Samuel Fuller has disowned *Shark* because he could not accept the producers' version of the film—presumably the version in release. But for its oddities, if not entirely for its qualities, *Shark,* no matter how mangled after it left Fuller's hands, still suggests the imagination that conceived, wrote and directed, for example,

An unidentified actor points the way in Shark. *Set in the Sudan, the movie was actually filmed in Mexico.*

ent are a drunken American doctor (Arthur Kennedy, a most engaging broad performance), a suspiciously omnipresent cop, and a cigar-smoking kid (Charles Berriochoa), with whom Reynolds forms a strong attachment.

It is typical of the film's perversions (on the gentle end of the scale) that although Reynolds has a little torrid beach sex with Miss Pinal, he flirts more with the kid,

Burt Reynolds and Arthur Kennedy.

Burt Reynolds and Silvia Pinal.

Underworld, U.S.A. (1960), *Shock Corridor* (1963), and *The Naked Kiss* (1964).

Set in the Sudan (but photographed in Mexico with a lot of local actors in secondary roles, so that whenever you aren't actually seeing a minaret or street bazaar, you tend to forget where you are supposed to be), *Shark* deals with a group of adventurers (Burt Reynolds, Barry Sullivan, and Silvia Pinal) engaged in recovering gold bullion from a ship sunk in the shark-infested waters of the Red Sea. Also pres-

*Underwater adventurers Burt, Barry
Sullivan, and Silvia Pinal.*

and the only shamelessly romantic shot has
Reynolds and the boy running toward each
other from a great distance along a sea
wall, to fall into each other's arms when
they are finally reunited.

On the less gentle end of the scale are
the whole system of relationships by be-
trayal (when her underwater colleagues
have finished retrieving the gold, Silvia
Pinal sends down bloody chunks of chopped

fish to excite the sharks—a lovely scene)
and that final sequence in which Miss
Pinal steams off into the glorious sunset,
the sole survivor, so she thinks—but with
her boat quietly flooding (Reynolds has
opened the seacocks) so that she will be
fed to other sharks and her treasure will,
of course, become the ruin of future adventurers.

The sharks are not merely symbolic;

they are not even problematic. They always show up (at least one always shows up, and it never fails to attack) and the sequences involving them are fine. However, the film's premise, that between the two environments, air and water, there is little to choose for predators, forces a weight of amorality on the leading players that none of them, in context, can adequately project.

With a relentless program of close-ups running through *Shark*—not for individual glamour but for intrusive presence— everyone emerges as a malevolent god of sorts. But nobody seems to have either the cold passion or the violent purpose that might certify his deification.

Burt hurls a length of chain into the face of Enrique Lucero.

FADE IN

"It should have been called **Fade Out.***"*
—*B.R.*

CREDITS

(Paramount—1968)
Producers, Judd Bernard, Silvio Narizzano; Associate Producer, Patricia Casey; Director, Jud Taylor; Screenwriter, Jerry Ludwig; Cinematographer, William Fraker; Editors, Aaron Stell, John W. Wheeler; Art Director, Albert Brenner; Music, Ken Lauber; Assistant Director, Louis Brandt; Running Time, 86 minutes

CAST

Rob, Burt Reynolds; *Jean,* Barbara Loden; *Pat,* Patricia Casey; *Russ,* Noam Pitlik; *Bud,* James Hampton; *George,* Joseph Perry; *Stu,* Lawrence Heller; *Phil,* Robert Sorrells; *Production Manager,* Steve Ferry; *Norman,* George Savalas; *Troy,* Wage Tucker; *Attendant,* Greg Robertson; *Sue Anne,* Sally Kirkland

Burt as Rob in Fade In.

Never shown in motion picture theaters, Fade In *was Burt's first full-scale love story.*

Burt Reynolds and Barbara Loden.

Filmed concurrently with Blue, Fade In *brought together* Blue *star Ricardo Montalban and* Fade In *star Reynolds.*

Mr. Reynolds tries to capture the attention of two young girls while waiting for his next scene.

Burt shows Blue star Terence Stamp a gun trick.

Burt and Barbara Loden silhouetted against a Utah sunset.

IMPASSE

"The title is my career at the time. It was a rough period."

—B.R.

CREDITS

(United Artists—1969)

Executive Producer, Aubrey Schenck; Producer, Hal Klein; Director, Richard Benedict; Screenwriter, John C. Higgins; Cinematographer, Mars B. Rasca; Editor, John F. Schreyer; Music, Philip Springer; Assistant Director, Donald Verk; Photographic Effects, Butler Glouner; Running Time, 100 minutes

CAST

Pat Morrison, Burt Reynolds; *Bobby Jones,* Anne Francis; *Hansen,* Lyle Bettger; *Draco,* Rodolfo Acosta; *Wombat,* Jeff Corey; *Trev*

Burt as Pat Morrison in Impasse.

Burt Reynolds and Anne Francis.

Jones, Clarke Gordon; *Mariko,* Miko Mayama; *Penny,* Joanne Dalsass; *Jesus,* Vic Diaz; *Pear Blossom,* Dely Atay-Atayan; *Nakajima,* Bruno Punzalan; *Maria Bonita,* Lily Campillos; *Sherry,* Shirley Gorospe; *Kiling,* Bessie Barredo; *Intern,* Robert Wang; *Kuli,* Eddie Nicart

PICK OF THE CRITICS
Jonathan Breslaw—*Motion Picture Herald*—May 21, 1969

"Crime doesn't pay" is the old-time moral which this Aubrey Schenck production uses for the occasion of a new exotic adventure film. But it is a sign of the times that *Impasse* does not imply condemnation of the crime itself (which is, after all, no more than larceny), but reproaches the participants for the human foibles which cause the caper to fail. The crime is in getting caught, is the half-jesting message of the picture. Ethical quibbles aside, *Impasse* packs plenty of action in a colorful Philippines setting, sticking to tried-and-true formulas for box-office success.

Burt Reynolds, a cynical young adventurer, finds out from Clarke Gordon, a broken-down former U.S. Army officer, that $3 million in gold hidden from the Japanese invaders during World War II remains buried on Corregidor Island. But to recover the loot, Reynolds must reunite the four men who helped bury it, now scattered all over the globe. He succeeds in this, but it seems that the four all hate each other's guts, so inner tensions are added to the tactical difficulty of stealing the gold from under the Philippine Army's eyes.

Reynolds soon gets together with Gordon's daughter Anne Francis, international tennis star, who is put off by Reynolds' mercenary cynicism but falls in love in spite of herself. Their affair annoys Miko Mayama, beautiful Japanese wife of one of the men involved in the plot, with whom Reynolds has a casual dalliance early in the picture. These dramatic com-

126

plications, added to the intricacies of the retrieval plans, make for some pretty confusing, if exciting action. Reynolds and the ex-soldiers resolve their differences enough to work their scheme, but they are foiled in the end by a tip-off from Miss Mayama, rejected and embittered. So Reynolds is punished not for his crime, but for fooling around with someone else's wife, and Miss Francis leaves the Philippines an older and wiser woman.

Reynolds, Misses Francis and Mayama perform well. Vic Diaz, Lyle Bettger, Rodolfo Acosta and Clarke Gordon are good as the quarrelsome ex-soldiers, and Jeff Corey is appropriately repellent as a slimy gossip columnist. Direction by Richard Benedict and screenplay by John C. Higgins are effective if cliché-ridden, and Mars B. Rasca's photography is attractive. *Impasse* makes for pretty good entertainment.

Burt Reynolds and Miko Mayama.

Burt Reynolds and Lyle Bettger.

Left to right: Lyle Bettger, Rodolfo Acosta, two unidentified soldiers, Burt Reynolds, Vic Diaz.

SAM WHISKEY

*"Way ahead of its time. I was playing
light comedy and nobody cared."*

—*B.R.*

CREDITS

(United Artists—1969)
Producers, Jules Levy, Arthur Gardner,
Arnold Laven; Director, Arnold Laven;
Screenwriter, William Norton; Cinematographer, Robert Moreno; Editor, John Woodcock; Art Director, Lloyd S. Papez; Set
Decorator, Charles Thompson; Music, Herschel Burke Gilbert; Assistant Director,
Burt Astor; Running Time, 96 minutes

CAST

Sam Whiskey, Burt Reynolds; *O.W. Bandy*,
Clint Walker; *Jedidiah Hooker*, Ossie
Davis; *Laura Breckinridge*, Angie
Dickinson; *Fat Henry Hobson*, Rick Davis;
Fisherman, Del Reeves; *Superintendent Perkins*, William Schallert; *Thornton Bromley*,
Woodrow Parfrey; *Cousin Leroy*, Anthony
James; *Hank*, John Damler; *Pete*, Bob
Adler; *The Blacksmith*, Chubby Johnson;
Big Annie, Ayllene Gibbons; *Mrs. Perkins*,
Amanda Harley

PICK OF THE CRITICS

John Mahoney—*Hollywood
Reporter*—February 3, 1969

Long on cunning and virtually bare of
violence, *Sam Whiskey* is an amiable western comedy, almost perfectly cast and fulfilling its modest pretensions and budget
with handy professionalism. Despite the occasional feeling that his television tenure
has included too much commercials viewing
and the tendency to anticipate their ultimate insertion in the film with Kleenex-pastoral interludes, Arnold Laven's
direction is his best since "Vice Squad,"
with a fine facility for playing out information in smooth pans and tracking shots and

Burt as the title star of Sam Whiskey.

an affinity for understated scenes and underplayed humor. The lean and likable script is by William Norton, who penned L/G/L's *Scalphunters* success last year, and Burt Reynolds' performance of the poker-playing, hard-fighting comic virgin of the title is just cause for a repeat turn. Overall, the film is no more, no less, than an elaborated segment of "The Wild, Wild West," equally light entertainment which may anticipate a healthy run and profits.

Reynolds enters into exhausting negotiations with Angie Dickinson, the widow of an ambitious politician, who seeks to have

Reynolds retrieve a quarter of a million dollars in gold bullion from a sunken steamboat at the bottom of the Platte River. Reynolds is then to replace the gold, which was to have financed an aborted rebellion, in the Denver mint and smuggle out the gilded lead bars which were placed in the vaults and will be detected when the minting of new coins begins. His resistance lowered by a night of persuasion and the promise of $20,000, Reynolds enlists blacksmith Ossie Davis and inventor Clint Walker to aid in the salvage and reverse-theft. Trailing them for the gold and ham-

Burt and Angie Dickinson. Mr. Reynolds has an enlargement of this photo hanging over his home bar. Under it he has humorously printed: "An Actor's Life Is Pure Hell!"

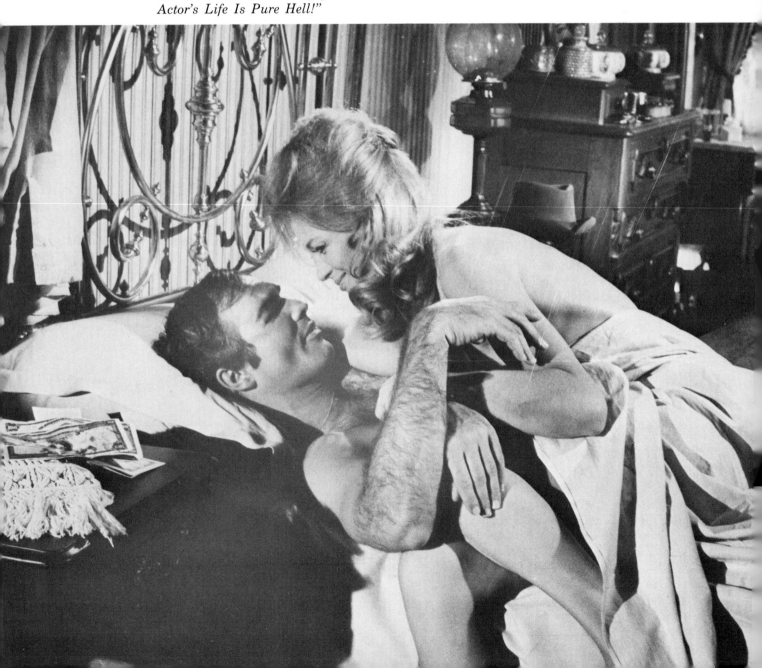

pering their success is the Fat Man, Rick Davis, and a band of dim-wit cutthroats borrowed at a price from ringmistress Ayllene Gibbons.

Impersonating a mint inspector, who is held bound and gagged and amused in a checkers tournament with Miss Dickinson, Reynolds gains entrance to the mint, gets the vault combination, key impressions and devises a ruse for smuggling out the gold and smelting it into bars under the noses of night watchmen. While there is plenty of hand to hand knockabout and a fusillade here and there, Laven manages never to show a direct hit or death. When Reynolds pans the mountainside with a homemade gatling gun to save his confederates, the mountain boys ostensibly just scatter and disappear, no need to view the carnage.

Miss Dickinson's extended persuasion in the buff and between the sheets, a comic sequence, is handled with such taste that one might assume that the couple is doing pushups, with Reynolds flaking out first. In all but those encounters relying on sheer cunning, the charm of Reynolds' Whiskey characterization is that he has more guts than staying power, though in fact Reynolds can handle a greater share of the rough stuff on screen than most of his contemporaries.

Burt gets a hot seat and ...

Left to right: Clint Walker, Ossie Davis, Burt Reynolds.

. . . a cooling off.

Ossie Davis has less to do in this film than one might hope, but gives a reliably fine performance. The surprise of the film, however, is Walker, playing against his size with bangs, spectacles and a studious bear-gentle manner, like a Royal Dano with an overactive pituitary. This inspired bit of casting and the natural humor which Walker extracts from it should spur imaginations which have not scratched this actor's comic promise since *Send Me No Flowers.*

Miss Dickinson has been encouraged to play her lines to good effect like a meller school marm, one who might be expected to seduce her way out of a mortgage.

Rick Davis, as the potential hijacker with paperweight glasses reminiscent of *Dr. Cyclops,* and William Schallert, as the dust-fingering mint superintendent, provide solid support.

Robert Moreno's photography, a serviceable score by Herschel Burke Gilbert and introductory tintype and stereopticon slide titles by Phill Norman, with crackerbarrel voice-over narration by Virgil Warner, greatly aid the easy style of this highly playable programer.

Clint, Burt, and Ossie pose for . . .

. . . publicity gag shots that . . .

Burt: "After my scenes with Angie, I donated the salary to charity. What a lovely lady!"

. . . were later killed.

100 RIFLES

*"I was an Indian with a mustache . . .
Raquel Welch on one side of me and Jim
Brown on the other. Jimmy was afraid of
only two things in the entire
world—heights and horses. And there he
was on a horse fighting me on a cliff."*
—B.R.

CREDITS

(20th Century-Fox—1969)
Producer, Marvin Schwartz; Director, Tom
Gries; Screenwriters, Clair Huffaker, Tom
Gries based on a novel, *The Californio*, by
Robert MacLeod; Cinematographer, Cecilio
Paniagua; Editor, Robert Simpson; Art Di-
rector, Carl Anderson; Music, Jerry Gold-
smith; Assistant Director, Tony Tarruella;
Photographic Effects, L.B. Abbott, Art
Cruickshank; Mechanical Effects, Alex
Weldon; Running Time, 110 minutes

CAST

Lyedecker, Jim Brown; *Sarita*, Raquel
Welch; *Yaqui Joe*, Burt Reynolds; *Verdugo*,
Fernando Lamas; *Grimes*, Dan O'Herlihy;
Von Klemme, Hans Gudegast; *Humara*, Mi-
chael Forest; *Sergeant Paletes*, Aldo
Sanbrell; *Girl in Hotel*, Soledad Miranda;
Padre Francisco, Alberto Dalbes; *Lopez*,
Carlos Bravo; *Sarita's Father*, Jose Manuel
Martin

PICK OF THE CRITICS

Mandel Herbstman—*Film Daily*—March 26,
1969

An outdoor action drama of muscular,
obstreperous proportions is pounded out in
100 Rifles. This Marvin Schwartz production for 20th Century-Fox bounces along
from adventure to adventure adding up to
rousing fare of a popular nature. There are
formula touches and fresh touches in the
screenplay that Clair Huffaker and Tom
Gries based on a novel by Robert MacLeod.
The film's cast is headed by Jim Brown,
Raquel Welch, Burt Reynolds, Fernando
Lamas and Dan O'Herlihy.

The story is set in Mexico at a time of
Indian oppression and rebellion. Brown
plays an American police officer who rides
into Mexico in hot pursuit of Reynolds, an
Indian bank robber. The tone of the violence to come is indicated by the first view
of Nogales, Mexico, where corpses dangle

Burt as Yaqui Joe in 100 Rifles.

Burt Reynolds and Raquel Welch.

from telephone poles as an example to revolutionary Yaqui Indians. It seems the local military governor, Lamas, has a unique way of solving the Indian problem. He kills them.

Brown catches up with his man but it's like getting the proverbial tiger by the tail. Since Reynolds is involved in the Indian uprisings Brown reluctantly gets involved too. The money from the bank robbery was used by Reynolds to buy 100 rifles for the Indians. Now there is the task of transporting the rifles to the Indians.

Miss Welch plays a revolutionary with a romantic attention to Reynolds that is later directed to Brown. Rounding out the cast is Dan O'Herlihy, an American businessman who runs the railroad.

Brown is determined to get Reynolds back to the U.S. as a prisoner. Towards this end Brown helps Reynolds slip away from Lamas' capture. Off they ride but both are caught. It looks like the firing squad for them but suddenly an army of Indians swoops down and rescues the pair.

Throughout the story there are killings of Indians by Lamas and his men. Gradu-

Yaqui Joe is detained by a Mexican soldier.

135

ally Brown gets drawn into the fight on the side of the Indians. Brown soon becomes the fighting hero of the Yaquis.

There is a fiery climax in which Lamas and his cruel henchmen are bumped off. Brown has a brief romance with Miss Welch but that is brought to an end by her death during a battle.

Gries' direction puts its accent on action. The photography by Cecilio Paniagua and the music by Jerry Goldsmith are both good.

Left to right: Burt Reynolds, Jim Brown, Hans Gudegast, Fernando Lamas.

Reynolds and Brown fight dirty on the edge of a steep mountain cliff.

Burt, Raquel, and Jim make an
exit—the hard way—in 100 Rifles.

SKULLDUGGERY

*"Nobody knew how to sell the picture.
When you have Pat Suzuki dressed as a
small ape, you're in trouble."*

—*B.R.*

Burt as Douglas Temple in
Skullduggery.

CREDITS

(Universal—1970)
Producer, Saul David; Associate Producer, Martin Fink; Director, Gordon Douglas; Screenwriter, Nelson Gidding; Cinematographer, Robert Moreno; Editor, John Woodcock; Production Designer, Hilyard Brown; Set Decorator, George Milo; Music, Oliver Nelson; Assistant Director, Bill Lukather; Special Effects, John Wallace Hyde; Running Time, 105 minutes

CAST

Douglas Temple, Burt Reynolds; *Sybil Greame*, Susan Clark; *Kreps*, Roger C. Carmel; *Vancruysen*, Paul Hubschmid; *Pop*, Chips Rafferty; *Buffington*, Alexander Knox; *Topazia*, Pat Suzuki; *Spofford*, Edward Fox; *Eaton*, Wilfrid Hyde-White; *Attorney General*, William Marshall; *Judge Draper*, Rhys Williams; *Dr. Figgins*, Mort Marshall; *Tee Hee*, Michael St. Clair; *Smoot*, Booker Bradshaw

Burt Reynolds and Susan Clark.

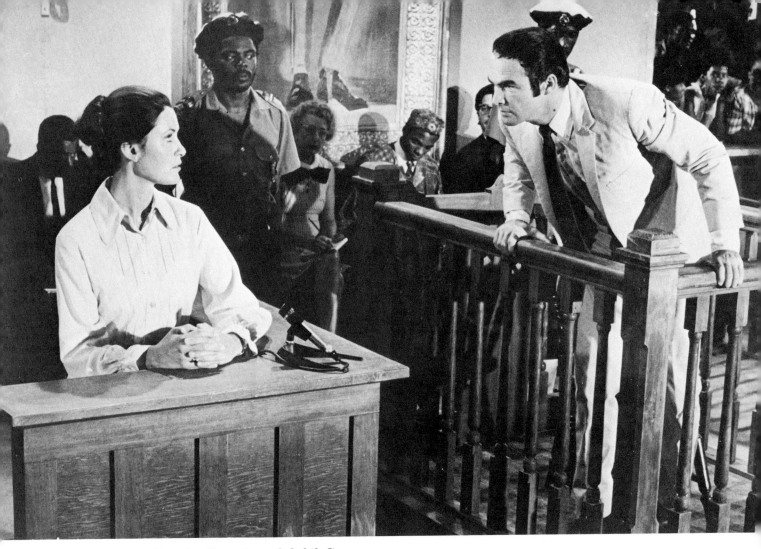

Douglas Temple and Sybil Greame
face each other in a New Guinea
courtroom.

Ex-footballer Burt throws a few passes
during his lunch break.

PICK OF THE CRITICS
Bernard Drew—*Hartford Times*—March 23,
1970

Skullduggery is a cheery, sometimes
mindless, occasionally quite high-minded
adventure spoof that goes in many directions.

It begins in the time-honored *King Kong*
tradition, with two engaging rascals joining
a scientific expedition in New Guinea,
headed by a prim lady in whom beats the
heart of a girl not quite so prim, and a
Catholic priest. They wish to discover the
missing link between man and ape.

There is a nice, casual raffish air to the
beginning which makes one hope that
Skullduggery is going to be this year's *The
Southern Star,* that small African gem of
last season which starred George Segal and
Orson Welles.

While the scientists are looking for ape
men, the two rascals are secretly searching
for phosphor, a rare mineral used in color
TV sets, and the nice-looking rascal and
the prim scientist are soon kitchy-kooing
behind the nets.

Left to right: Roger C. Carmel, Burt Reynolds, Susan Clark.

Future director Reynolds takes a behind-the-camera look at Skullduggery.

Then they come upon a settlement of Tropis, small, cute ape men and women, led by a bearded Pat Suzuki and very charming she is as a kind of simian Myrna Loy.

Pretty soon, it is discovered that the Tropis are the cheapest labor on earth, and a syndicate led by an evil Dutchman moves in and takes over everything—including the lady scientist.

All this is rather fun, but now comes the moral question: are these Tropis apes or human; are they white or black? And the screenplay by Nelson Gidding giddily alternates between high social seriousness and zany humor, ending, inconclusively, with a mad Scopes trial.

It's rather silly, but I enjoyed a lot of it.

Gordon Douglas directed, and the likable cast is headed by Burt Reynolds, who is excellent as one of the rascals; Susan Clark, fine as the lady scientist; and Roger C. Carmel as the other rascal, which he plays like a Boer Walter Brennan. Chips Rafferty, Paul Hubschmid, Alexander Knox, Wilfrid Hyde-White, and William Marshall are some of the other good people involved.

FUZZ

"It was kind of fuzzy."

—B.R.

CREDITS
(United Artists—1972)
Executive Producer, Edward S. Feldman; Producer, Jack Farren; Associate Producer, Charles H. Maguire; Director, Richard A. Colla; Screenwriter, Evan Hunter from a novel by Ed McBain; Cinematographer, Jacques Marquette; Editor, Robert Kimble; Art Director, Hilyard Brown; Set Decorator, Philip Abramson; Music, Dave Grusin; Assistant Director, Arthur Levinson; Running Time, 93 minutes

Burt as Steve Carella and Neile Adams as Teddy Carella in Fuzz.

CAST

Detective Steve Carella, Burt Reynolds; *Detective Meyer Meyer*, Jack Weston; *Detective Bert Kling*, Tom Skerritt; *The Deaf Man*, Yul Brynner; *Detective Eileen McHenry*, Raquel Welch; *Detective Arthur Brown*, James McEachin; *Detective Andy Parker*, Steve Ihnat; *Detective Hal Willis*, Stewart Moss; *Lieutenant Byrnes*, Dan Frazer; *Sergeant Murchison*, Bert Remsen; *Buck*, Peter Bonerz; *Ahmad*, Cal Bellini; *Anthony La Bresca*, Don Gordon; *Pete Scroeder*, Charles Tyner; *Jimmy*, Gary Morgan; *Teddy Carella*, Neile Adams

PICK OF THE CRITICS

Charles Michener—*Newsweek*—July 31, 1972

If there is such a thing as the perfect "hammock movie," *Fuzz* is it—a shaggy-dog, cops-and-robbers comedy with as much refeshing garbage in it as a planter's punch. Most of it is shameless rip-off. When he isn't dressing up like a bum to nab some teen-agers who like to set fire to derelicts, Detective Steve Carella (Burt Reynolds) is dressing up like a nun to foil the mysterious, deaf killer of city officials —with a lack of finesse that makes *The French Connection*'s Popeye Doyle look like Sherlock Holmes. Spice is provided by none

Burt catches vandal Gary Morgan.

In search of a murderer, Carella pretends to be a skid row bum.

other than Raquel Welch as a straight-arrow woman detective who takes a ribbing from the squadroom sexists. And we get Yul Brynner as the wicked Deaf Man, reminiscent of the bizarre villains in the old Bond movies, complete with guttural accent, technological wizardry, and a statuesque, piano-playing black girlfriend who can't get the notes right in "Heart and Soul."

Based on one of Ed McBain's 87th Precinct novels, transplanted from Manhattan to Boston, the film is fuzzy on suspense but razor-bright in wit—thanks to the agreeable thick-headedness of Reynolds, the boyish Tom Skerritt, and the marshmallow toughness of Jack Weston as Detective Meyer Meyer. Sometimes the humor goes flat-footed—as when Miss Welch tries to untangle herself from a stake-out in a   143

*Disguised as nuns, undercover police-
men Burt Reynolds and Jack Weston
patrol the Boston Common.*

sleeping bag. But director Richard A. Colla
is unusually deft at making the point that
cops may be more victimized than the vic-
tims they are supposed to protect. And
screenwriter Evan Hunter (the real "Ed
McBain") time and again tracks down his
man—as in the moment when a rookie cop
takes a call from a woman who's being
molested, puts her on hold, and turns to
ask: "What shall I tell her?"

DELIVERANCE

"It's the best film I've ever done. It's a picture that just picks you up and crashes you against the rocks. You feel everything and just crawl out of the theater. It was beautifully cast and fabulously directed. Vilmos Zsigmond, the cinematographer, wasn't nominated for an Oscar—a great example of how stupid the Academy of Motion Picture Arts and Sciences can be."

—B.R.

Burt as Lewis in Deliverance.

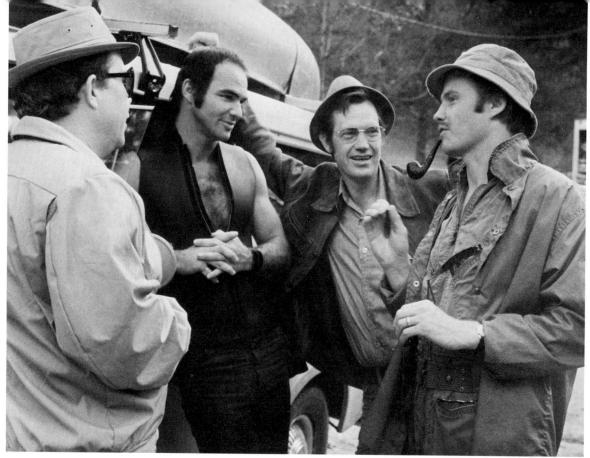

Left to right: Ned Beatty, Burt Reynolds, Ronny Cox, Jon Voight.

CREDITS
(Warner Brothers—1972)

Producer/Director, John Boorman; Screenwriter, James Dickey based on his novel; Cinematographer, Vilmos Zsigmond; Editor, Tom Priestley; Art Director, Fred Harpman; Music, Eric Weissberg; Assistant Director, Al Jennings; Special Effects, Marcel Vercoutere; Technical Advisers, Charles Wiggin, E. Lewis King; Running Time, 109 minutes

CAST

Ed, Jon Voight; *Lewis,* Burt Reynolds; *Bobby,* Ned Beatty; *Drew,* Ronny Cox; *Mountain Man,* Billy McKinney; *Toothless Man,* Herbert "Cowboy" Coward; *Sheriff Bullard,* James Dickey; *Old Man,* Ed Ramey; *Lonny,* Billy Redden; *1st Grinner,* Seamon Glass; *2nd Grinner,* Randall Deal; *1st Deputy,* Lewis Crone; *2nd Deputy,* Ken Keener; *Ambulance Driver,* Johnny Popwell; *Doctor,* John Fowler; *Nurse,* Kathy Rickman; *Mrs. Biddiford,* Louise Coldren; *Taxi Driver,* Pete Ware; *Boy at Gas Station,* Hoyt J. Pollard; *Martha Gentry,* Belinha Beatty; *Ed's Boy,* Charlie Boorman

PICK OF THE CRITICS
Arthur Knight—*Saturday Review*—August 5, 1972

Deliverance, which James Dickey adapted from his own best-selling novel, is one of those rare films that resonates like a literary work but that—rarer still—avoids either being or sounding literary. For me a good book is one that does more than simply tell an arresting story; it creates characters who face moments of crisis and moral dilemma in which they must make choices. And the choices are not necessarily simple, obvious ones between wrong and right, good and evil. Life is generally far more complicated than that, and the novelist, reflecting life, must work these complexities into his design. When he does—as Dickey surely did in *Deliverance*—one is haunted long after the final chapter by what has happened to the characters as the result of a decision made under duress, what their lives might have been had the decision been different.

Similarly, a good film for me is one that doesn't end with final titles. Too many pictures are designed merely to amuse or entertain for an hour-and-a-half or so, then send you home unmoved, uninvolved, and unsatisfied. But there are other films that cling to the mind and somehow keep growing and expanding until the imagination itself supplies entire scenes that the film-maker merely hinted at. I suspect that *Deliverance* will prove to be such a film.

For one thing, the film is beautifully made. Director John Boorman, working in the remote, thickly wooded mountain country of northern Georgia—just as he did with Alcatraz in *Point Blank* and with that South Seas island in *Hell in the Pacific*—succeeds in plunging us promptly and deeply into an alien culture, an alien world. More so, I should say, in *Deliverance* than in any of his previous pictures. Even before the opening titles have cleared the screen while we are still watching two cars, canoes atop, penetrating unpaved mountain roads through dark, forbidding forests, the film starts to take effect. Although we have not yet seen the occupants of the cars, we half-hear their conversations and gather that they have driven up

A copy of this photo hangs in Mr. Reynolds' office. It is inscribed: "Burt, This is that moment when I suspect you are me—and handling it much better! Love, Jon."

147

from the city for a weekend of canoeing and camping in a wilderness that is about to be tamed. The bulldozers are already at work, readying ground for a dam that will transform this forest primeval into a placid lake.

What follows is perhaps the most extraordinary scene in American films of recent years. The cars pull up before an ancient shanty. The city men need drivers to deliver their cars to them downstream. They peek in the windows and see only a ravaged hag and a child dying of malnutrition. Another child, almost catatonic, sits vacantly in a swing on a collapsing porch. While a simpleton gasses up their cars, one of the city men strikes a few notes on his guitar. The child on the porch responds on his banjo. A few more notes, another response. In no time the two are challenging each other with bits of music. It is a contest that the child—empty-eyed, toothlessly grinning—wins easily. And immediately he returns to his catatonic state.

It is completely a movie moment, emphasizing at once the connections between the city people and the mountain people but, more especially, the gulf that separates them. Boorman again utilizes this moment when, as the men from the city paddle their canoes downstream, they pass under a wooden footbridge. The boy is watching them, and his vacant, impersonal stare creates a chill foreboding of the horror to come. The mountain men and the city men live in worlds apart.

Much of the film is sheer action. There are three canoe runs through the churning white waters of the Chattooga River, each with its own perils. With bow and arrow the men shoot fish, deer—and other men. And when they do so, *Deliverance* is sud-

Burt lost ten pounds and Jon Voight lost fifteen during the filming of Deliverance.

Lewis and Bobby versus the river.

denly transformed from a superior adventure movie into a picture that poses deep moral problems for each of its principals. Two of the city men, Jon Voight and Ned Beatty, have pulled their canoe ashore in advance of the others. Out of the silence of the forest two mountain men emerge and take them prisoners. The mountaineers torture one city man, bugger the other. The second canoe silently arrives, and Burt Reynolds, quickly assessing the situation, kills one of the mountaineers with an arrow. The other flees into the wilderness. Now what will these four civilized men do with the body? If they bring it downstream, what kind of justice will they receive from these closely knit mountain folk? On the other hand, the whole area will become a lake in a week or two, and, if they buried the dead man, who would know?

The journey downstream proceeds through another stretch of white water, and the guitar player (Ronny Cox) tumbles out of the canoe. Was he shot by the mountaineer who escaped? Voight assumes that the party is being shadowed and climbs a sharp precipice to bring down their pursuer. Lying in ambush he lets fly an arrow at a man with a rifle. When he comes upon the body, however, he is unable to make the identification for certain. He may have killed an innocent man.

Deliverance doesn't attempt to answer questions. The rights or wrongs of what the city people did with the first mountaineer, the guilt or innocence of the second dead man, are left unresolved. As in the novel, the film bores in on the effects of these events upon the men involved. And it is this unresolved, open-ended quality that leaves the viewer haunted and unresolved in his own mind. What would I have done if I had been there?

To make all of this unremittingly persuasive, Boorman took his small, carefully selected cast into the actual locations of Dickey's horror tale and shot in complete continuity. Whatever the extra costs—in human suffering as well as money—it was worth it. Reynolds registers as he never has before as the headstrong, self-assured

149

Lewis is seriously wounded.

organizer of the expedition; Voight effectively underplays as his mild-mannered, pipe-smoking friend who enjoys an occasional taste of the wilds. The camera work by Vilmos Zsigmond is impeccable, and the score—banjo and guitar—is mercifully minimal. Dickey encounters some difficulty in unraveling the several skeins of his story in the final reel, but no matter. Everything that has gone before is so powerful, so right, that any attempt at a neat solution could cause only resentment. After the fade-out, the mind takes over. Which is as it should be.

Left to right: Ned Beatty, Bill McKinney, Burt Reynolds, Jon Voight.

Director John Boorman (center) gives instructions to his actors before tackling another dangerous scene.

James Dickey, author of both the novel and the screenplay, portrays Sheriff Bullard in Deliverance; *with him are Jon Voight, Burt, and Ned Beatty.*

EVERTHING YOU ALWAYS WANTED TO KNOW ABOUT SEX

"I did my part in one day. Woody Allen is very serious. He likes it absolutely quiet on the set, no craziness. I would like to work with him again."

—B.R.

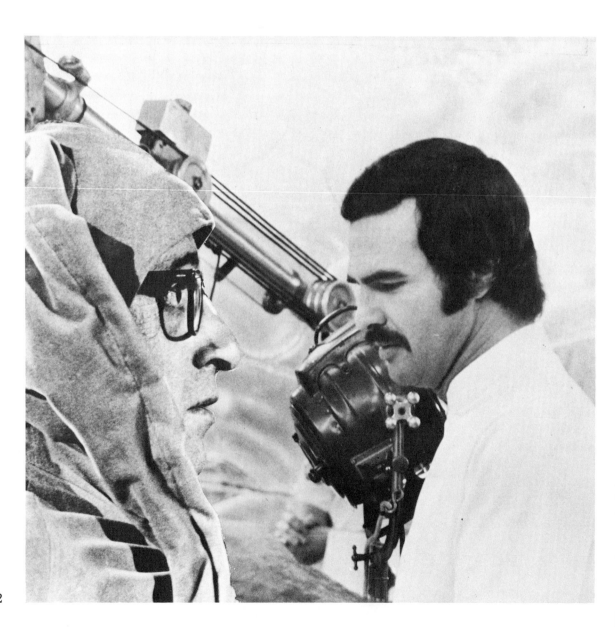

CREDITS
(United Artists—1972)
Executive Producer, Jack Brodsky; Producer, Charles H. Joffe; Associate Producer, Jack Grossberg; Director/Screenwriter, Woody Allen based on the book by Dr. David Reuben; Cinematographer, David M. Walsh; Editors, James T. Heckert, Eric Albertson; Production Designer, Dale Hennesy; Set Decorator, Marvin March; Music, Mundell Lowe; Assistant Director, Fred T. Gallo; Running Time, 88 minutes

CAST
Victor, Fabrizio, The Fool, Sperm, Woody Allen; *Dr. Bernardo,* John Carradine; *Sam,* Lou Jacobi; *Gina,* Louise Lasser; *The King,* Anthony Quayle; *The Operator,* Tony Randall; *The Queen,* Lynn Redgrave; *Switchboard,* Burt Reynolds; *Dr. Ross,* Gene Wilder; *Himself,* Jack Barry; *The Girl,* Erin Fleming; *Mrs. Ross,* Elaine Giftos; *Herself,* Toni Holt; *Himself,* Robert Q. Lewis; *Helen,* Heather MacRae; *George,* Sidney Miller; *Herself,* Pamela Mason; *Himself,* Regis Philbin; *Milos,* Titos Vandis; *Stomach Operator,* Stanley Adams; *Brain Control,* Oscar Beregi; *The Fool's Father,* Alan Caillou; *Sheriff,* Dort Clark; *Sorcerer,* Geoffrey Holder; *The Priest,* Jay Robinson; *Igor,* Ref Sanchez; *1st Football Player,* Don Chuy; *Rabbi Baumel,* Baruch Lumet; *2nd Football Player,* Tom Mack; *Sperm,* Robert Walden; *Bernard Jaffe,* H.E. West

PICK OF THE CRITICS
William Wolf—*Cue*—August 12, 1972

All hail, Woody Allen. He has taken topics in Dr. David Reuben's best-seller and, providing his own elaborations, has made a hysterically funny and imaginative comedy. This is more than just horseplay. In what is certainly his best, most cohesive work, Allen creates the modern equivalent of Boccaccio's bawdy tales. Sex is spoofed with far greater wit, sophistication, and comic insight than in any film I've experienced. What happens during ejaculation? You'll find Woody Allen as a sperm, waiting with his fellow sperm for the mighty call, while a research crew who look like they're at Cape Canaveral prepare for launching. Perversion is covered in the funniest TV parody I've seen—a program called "What's My Perversion?" Sodomy is explored, with Gene Wilder as a doctor stunned at the problem of a man in love with his sheep—until he meets the sheep. There's a great parody of Italian movies with Allen as a man faced with a wife who has trouble having orgasms—except in public places, and a memorable parody of horror films in a sex-research segment, as a giant breast breaks loose from the laboratory to terrorize the countryside. The remarkable thing is that Allen isn't obscene, just cleverly risque, as he masterfully satirizes movies, TV, and literature while having fun with sex.

Burt makes a brief appearance in Woody Allen's Everything You Always Wanted to Know About Sex.

SHAMUS

"Not a bad film, kind of cute. If the picture had been as good as the title sequence, it would have made big millions. As it was, it made a few million."

—B.R.

CREDITS
(Columbia—1973)
Producer, Robert M. Weitman; Associate Producer, Jim Di Gangi; Director, Buzz Kulik; Screenwriter, Barry Beckerman; Cinematographer, Victor J. Kemper; Editor, Walter Thompson; Art Director, Philip Rosenberg; Set Decorator, Edward Stewart; Music, Jerry Goldsmith; Assistant Director, Ted Zachary; Running Time, 98 minutes

CAST
McCoy, Burt Reynolds; *Alexis*, Dyan Cannon; *Colonel Hardcore*, John Ryan; *Lieutenant Promuto*, Joe Santos; *Dottore*, Georgio Tozzi; *Hume*, Ron Weyand; *Springy*, Larry

Burt Reynolds and Ron Weyand.

Burt as Shamus McCoy in Shamus.

Block; *Bolton,* Beeson Carroll; *The Kid,* Kevin Conway; *Bookstore Girl,* Kay Frye; *Johnnie,* John Glover; *Schnook,* Merwin Goldsmith; *Woman,* Melody Santangelo; *Heavy,* Irving Selbst; *Felix,* Alex Wilson; *The Cat,* Morris; *Willie,* Tony Amato, Jr.; *Rock,* Lou Martell; *Dealer,* Marshall Anker; *Doorman,* Bert Bertram; *Drifter,* Jimmy Kelly; *Hatcheck Girl,* Alisha Fontaine; *Pimp,* Mickey Freeman; *Handler,* Captain Arthur Haggerty

PICK OF THE CRITICS
Alan R. Howard—*Hollywood Reporter*—January 31, 1973

Actor Burt Reynolds and director Buzz Kulik turn cartweels and backflips to give Robert M. Weitman's production, *Shamus,* substance and locomotion. Fortunately, both are so resourceful that the handsomely produced movie is funny and entertaining despite the screenplay's faulty structure.

Reynolds' fresh sense of humor about himself is totally appropriate for the private eye he plays. This guy is no James Bond, he's a real human being who even feels fear. Reynolds' athletic performance is consistently amusing, and the force of his

Tommy Lane, Burt, and a bloody Alex Wilson make an escape. Burt is wearing knee pads, indicating that he did his own stunt work in the scene.

personality has never been better used in a movie.

Reynolds' likability almost excuses the unpleasant violence his character occasionally uses to obtain information. Since so much of *Shamus* is a tribute to Bogart, it's surprising the filmmakers didn't remember that Bogart never tortured anyone.

Kulik creates a series of authentic milieus; his work has energy, wit, visual flair and the breath of life in it. He pumps vitality into his scenes without turning the movie into a three-ring circus. His action scenes have a graceful control in them which truly tests his mettle as a director.

Burt Reynolds and Dyan Cannon.

Burt decks heavy Arthur Haggerty.

Dyan Cannon, who is top-billed with Reynolds, has little to do but laugh and smile. It's a shame because her sultry, knowing presence is perfect for the genre. To her credit, the actress takes the movie away whenever she's on screen.

Writer Barry Beckerman's dialogue is sometimes witty and thanks to Reynolds, much of the movie is funny. But *Shamus* has no coherent story to tell and doesn't bother to explore the relationships between

Shamus was filmed at eighteen never-used-before location sites—among them a suburban cement company—in and around New York City.

its characters. Sometimes it's impossible to know what's going on.

Scenes from famous private-eye movies flow gratuitously into *Shamus*. The movie repeats, for example, Bogart's famous tryst with Dorothy Malone in a bookstore from *The Big Sleep*. Actress Kaye Frye is certainly beautiful and enticing, but such detours might puzzle non-film buff audiences.

Reynolds is hired by a multi-millionaire eccentric (Ron Weyand) to find out who stole some jewels he owns. His search is aided by Springy, brilliantly played by Larry Block, a nervous, little guy who memorizes world's records. Dyan Cannon's brother, a former football star played by Alex Wilson, is not only involved with the theft but also in the illegal purchase of weapons from yet another screen spoof of a crazed military man (John Ryan).

Georgio Tozzi appears briefly and magnificently as a mafia chieftain with a finely developed palate for gourmet foods. Joe Santos is fine as a hard-nosed detective.

The production itself is consistently fresh and exciting, with an engaging selection of unusual locations, secondary characters and extras. Victor J. Kemper's photography is properly harsh without being unattractive, a difficult balance to achieve. Film editor Walter Thompson's craftsmanship is a lesson in technique and control.

WHITE LIGHTNING

"I think it's an excellent example of a picture that is everything it tries to be—no more, no less. I liked it a lot."

—B.R.

CREDITS
(United Artists—1973)
Producers, Arthur Gardner, Jules Levy; Director, Joseph Sargent; Screenwriter, William Norton; Cinematographer, Edward Rosson; Editor, George Nicholson; Music, Charles Bernstein; Assistant Director, Edward Teets; Special Effects, Cliff Wenger; Running Time, 101 minutes

CAST
Gator McKlusky, Burt Reynolds; *Lou,* Jennifer Billingsley; *Sheriff Connors,* Ned Beatty; *Roy Boone,* Bo Hopkins; *Dude Watson,* Matt Clark; *Martha Culpepper,* Louise Latham; *Maggie,* Diane Ladd; *Big Bear,* R.G. Armstrong; *Deputy,* Conlan Carter; *Pa McKlusky,* Dabbs Greer; *Superintendent Simms,* Lincoln Demyan; *Skeeter,* John Steadman; *Ma McKlusky,* Iris Korn; *Jenny,* Stephanie Burchfield; *Louella,* Barbara Muller; *Harvey,* Robert Ginnaven; *Sister Linda Fay,* Fay Martin; *1st Treasury Agent,* Richard Allin; *2nd Treasury Agent,* Bill Bond; *Junior,* Glenn Wilder; *1st Highway Patrolman,* Dick Ziker; *2nd Highway Patrolman,* Buddy Joe Hooker; *Student,* Kathy Finley; *Sherry Lynn,* Sherry Boucher

PICK OF THE CRITICS
Charles Champlin—*Los Angeles Times*—August 16, 1973

Burt Reynolds continues to emerge as one of the most watchable and versatile personalities in the movies. He moves easily from brute action to intense feeling and from light comedy to dark romance. His *Sam Whiskey* was a nifty low-comedy western which deserved more attention than it got, and the brooding strength of his performance in *Deliverance* revealed a fine dramatic actor at work.

Burt as Gator McKlusky in White Lightning.

In *White Lightning,* a fast and furious adventure which opens citywide today, Reynolds delivers a varied, screen-commanding star turn which is a pleasure to watch. The movie, directed by Joseph Sargent from an original script by William Norton, is that scarce commodity, a stirring, satisfying summer-weight entertainment.

Reynolds is a demon driver doing time for running moonshine, an easygoing country boy who gets himself released from a Southern state prison to make a case against the crooked sheriff who has murdered Reynolds' kid brother.

Burt Reynolds and Jennifer Billingsley.

Left to right: Burt Reynolds, R.G. Armstrong, Conlan Carter.

He gets little help from another parolee-informer (Matt Clark), but he infiltrates the bootleg business through another runner (Bo Hopkins). The trail leads from the still-man (R.G. Armstrong), right to the sheriff, who is played with malevolent cornpone authenticity by Ned Beatty, the same (if unrecognizable) actor who went canoeing with Reynolds in *Deliverance.*

There are some steamy diversions, principally provided by Jennifer Billingsley as Hopkins' sluttish girlfriend who takes a shine to the new moonshiner and by Louise Latham as the sheriff's up-tight spinster secretary.

At a point at which you'd have said the

car chase caper must be played out, *White*

Gator (Burt) and Lou (Jennifer) hug and scrub on a hot Southern afternoon.

Lightning proves it isn't. There are two chases, in fact, both ingenious autobatic sequences which lead to soaring, incredible finishes.

Reynolds, abetted by Norton's sharp, accurate dialogue, creates a vivid character —tough, earnest, sardonic, crafty, and also sensitive. He carries his weight in the

Second unit director Hal Needham shows prisoner Burt how to punch out a deputy (Glenn Wilder).

Jennifer Billingsley, Matt Clark, and Burt Reynolds.

Bo Hopkins and Burt in a realistic fight scene.

brawlings, but he also lets you know the shame he feels at being a stool pigeon, even in a good cause. William Faulkner it was never intended to be, but Reynolds lends unexpected dimensions to a straight-out melodramatic role.

The swampy execution of the kid brother and a fellow civil rights demonstrator takes place in silence behind the main titles and quickly establishes the sullen and ominous setting for the action to follow. The script observes the dramatic unities to a fare-thee-well, which is one of the satisfactions of the movie.

The acting is first-rate throughout. Beyond the excellent principals, there is notably fine work by Diane Ladd as Matt Clark's wife, Conlan Carter as a crooked deputy and Lincoln Demyan as the boss of the prison farm.

Charles Bernstein did the effective music and Edward Rosson's cinematography catches the look and the feel of the moonshine country (the actual locations were in Arkansas). Sargent's direction lets the fast-moving story seem to tell itself, which is something these tricky days, but the incisive performances are anything but accidental.

White Lightning is a highly professional piece of work, swift and suspenseful, with a good sense of time, place and ominous atmosphere.

Burt Reynolds, Sr.; Burt Reynolds, Jr.; and Dinah Shore on the Arkansas location of White Lightning.

THE MAN WHO LOVED CAT DANCING

"Cat Dancing was sorrow and pain. I'd rather not talk about it."

—B.R.

CREDITS
(Metro-Goldwyn-Mayer—1973)

Producers, Martin Poll, Eleanor Perry; Associate Producer, Ted W. Sewell; Director, Richard C. Sarafian; Screenwriter, Eleanor Perry based on the novel by Marilyn Durham; Cinematographer, Harry Stradling, Jr.; Editor, Tom Rolf; Art Director, Edward C. Carfagno; Set Decorator, Ralph S. Hurst; Music, John Williams; Assistant Director, Les Sheldon; Running Time, 114 minutes

Burt Reynolds and Sarah Miles.

Burt as Jay Grobart in The Man Who Loved Cat Dancing.

Left to right: Bo Hopkins, Sarah Miles, Burt Reynolds, Jack Warden.

Burt incurred an abdominal hernia during this fight scene with Jack Warden.

CAST

Jay Grobart, Burt Reynolds; *Catherine Crocker*, Sarah Miles; *Lapchance*, Lee J. Cobb; *Dawes*, Jack Warden; *Crocker*, George Hamilton; *Billy*, Bo Hopkins; *Dub*, Robert Donner; *Ben*, Sandy Kevin; *Iron Knife*, Larry Littlebird; *Sudie*, Nancy Malone; *The Chief*, Jay Silverheels; *Charlie*, Jay Varela; *Grobart's Son*, Sutero Garcia, Jr.

PICK OF THE CRITICS

Roger Ebert—*Chicago Sun-Times*—June 29, 1973

The Man Who Loved Cat Dancing begins as a movie about an armed train robbery and ends as a curiously affecting love story. And somehow it moves from point A to point B with such logic and grace that we accept the change in emphasis and are grateful for it; this isn't just another violent western.

The man in the title is played by Burt Reynolds, and Cat Dancing was his Indian wife, killed some years before. He was a respected and loved captain in the U.S. Army during the Civil War, but now he's gotten himself involved in the train-robbery scheme: he has some hazy plans to use the money to buy back his two children, who live with their native tribe.

The train robbery goes off smoothly enough except that the gang inadvertently captures a rancher's wife (Sarah Miles) and takes her along for nefarious purposes. Reynolds himself hardly notices the girl for the first hour of the movie; but then a relationship grows between them, rough and tentative at first but finally based on a shared desperation. The way their love develops, slowly and almost unwillingly, is the best thing in this line since the Charlton Heston–Joan Hackett romance in *Will Penny*.

Director Richard Sarafian and writer Eleanor Perry achieve a nice elegiac tone in the last half of the movie without laying another one of those death-of-the-West themes on us. Their West is still alive enough, but it provides vast empty spaces and long silences during which old memories become obsessive. The Reynolds character is a terribly lonely man, but an essentially good one; and the woman is not so much escaping her sadistic husband (George Hamilton) as running toward the strength she feels from Reynolds.

The movie was based on the best-selling novel by Marilyn Durham (an Evansville, Indiana, housewife who, perhaps to her own astonishment, found her first book selected by the Book-of-the-Month Club). And Eleanor Perry's screenplay understands the novel's strength; that this is essentially a man-woman story, and the violence, the gunplay, and even the long chase have to be secondary to that. So the movie isn't breakneck; it's willing to settle down sometimes for the longer scenes necessary to establish a relationship.

One of the best of these occurs when Reynolds and Miles arrive at an abandoned mining camp and she cooks him dinner. He begins the dinner as the gruff, impervious type he's been all along, but they end it in each other's arms. The scene is played largely without dialogue, and depends mostly on Sarah Miles's eyes for its exposition. A lot of scenes have depended on less.

What's most surprising about *The Man Who Loved Cat Dancing* is probably the Reynolds performance. We knew Sarah Miles could act (as can Lee J. Cobb and Jack Warden, two other important cast

Jay Grobart (Burt) and Catherine Crocker (Sarah Miles) ride into a barren desert camp.

Burt Reynolds and Jay Silverheels.

Left to right: Burt Reynolds, Bo Hopkins, Sarah Miles, Nancy Malone.

members). But Reynolds, by his own admission, has appeared mostly in junk up until now. Even his performance in *Deliverance* emphasized only one aspect of the character. But now here's a very difficult dramatic role, and he's fine in it. And he finally gets over Cat Dancing.

Sarah Miles silently observes The Man Who Loved Cat Dancing.

THE LONGEST YARD

"I still wear a Longest Yard jersey around the house. It will always be a special film to me."

—B.R.

CREDITS
(Paramount—1974)
Producer, Albert S. Ruddy; Associate Producer, Alan P. Horowitz; Director, Robert Aldrich; Screenwriter, Tracy Keenan Wynn based on a story by Albert S. Ruddy; Cinematographer, Joseph Biroc; Editor, Michael Luciano; Production Designer, James S. Vance; Music, Frank De Vol; Assistant Director, Cliff Coleman, Jr.; Running Time, 121 minutes

CAST
Paul Crewe, Burt Reynolds; *Warden Hazen,* Eddie Albert; *Captain Knauer,* Ed Lauter; *Scarboro,* Michael Conrad; *Caretaker,* James Hampton; *Granville,* Harry Caesar; *Pop,* John Steadman; *Unger,* Charles Tyner; *Rasmeussen,* Mike Henry; *Walking Boss,* Joe Kapp; *Warden's Secretary,* Bernadette Peters; *Shop Steward,* Pepper Martin; *Spooner,* Ernie Wheelwright; *Rotka,* Tony Cacciotti; *Samson,* Richard Kiel; *Mawabe,* Pervis Atkins; *Mason,* Dino Washington; *Bogdanski,* Ray Nitschke; *Assistant Warden,* Mort Marshall; *Melissa,* Anitra Ford; *Announcer,* Michael Fox; *The Indian,* Sonny Sixkiller; *Shokner,* Robert Tessier; *Ice Man,* Jim Reynolds

PICK OF THE CRITICS
Art Murphy—*Daily Variety*—August 20, 1974

Robert Aldrich's career has been full of ups and downs, but boy, is he back on top again. *The Longest Yard* is an outstanding action drama, combining the brutish excite-

Burt as Paul Crewe in The Longest Yard.

ment of football competition with the brutalities of contemporary prison life. Burt Reynolds again asserts his genuine star power, here as a former football pro forced to field a team under blackmail of warden Eddie Albert. Tracy Keenan Wynn's excellent script has been produced most realistically and handsomely by Albert S. Ruddy. The Paramount release is a terrific commercial bet among all segments of the mass audience.

In contrast to most hard action films, this is quality action drama, in which brute force is fully motivated and therefore totally acceptable. At the same time, the metaphysics of football—that barbarous human power struggle which realizes the fantasies of fans and coaches at the expense of players' hides and health and dignity —are neatly interwoven with the politics and bestialities of totalitarian authority. Rotten films have reached for the ideas in *The Longest Yard,* and still more rotten films have shamelessly exploited the violence, but very few have ever combined the action and ideas so successfully.

Burt Reynolds and Anitra Ford.

Wynn's script, from a story credited to producer Ruddy, finds Reynolds tiring of being Anitra Ford's kept stud; she calls the cops when he splits in her car, provoking an early car chase (very well directed by Hal Needham) and eventual arrival at Albert's prison. Albert's placid mien has al-

Football star Paul Crewe throws his socialite girlfriend around; she has him thrown in prison.

Burt breaks up after a slippery encounter with Tony Cacciotti in the Georgia swamps.

Burt and James Hampton look over the recruits they have collected for the prison's football team.

ways had the potential for casting in a role of cold malice, and he does a terrific job.

Ed Lauter, his chief guard, also coaches the guards' clumsy football team. Reynolds is forced to form an inmates' team from a rag-tag bunch of cons, with a no-win payoff: if he loses, Lauter's guards will rub it in; if he wins, Albert's vengeance is certain.

A lot of prerelease hype has likened this film to Aldrich's *The Dirty Dozen* (a 1967 MGM picture which to date has thrown off domestic theatrical film rentals alone of about $20,250,000). There are, indeed, many genuine similarities. Then, too, the inner conflict of an athlete tempted to betraying his profession is a reminder of *Body and Soul*, a 1947 film on which Aldrich was the first assistant director. The buffs can take it from there.

It used to be said that all-male (or nearly so) action films could, if the machismo were laid on heavily enough, attract substantial female audiences. Even more so now, what with televised football, complete with instant replay, which has developed millions of femme fans. This film puts all that together into a surefire b.o. 167

Left to right: Ray Nitschke, Burt Reynolds, John Steadman.

package which, with due regard to the few new film hits, as well as the important-looking films breaking at the end of the year, could be among the highest-grossing pictures of 1974.

The extremely large cast excels everywhere. Besides Lauter's fine performance, Jim Hampton is superb as Reynolds' team manager, eventually killed by Charles Tyner, a stoolie in Lauter's employ. Michael Conrad is tops as Reynolds' coaching assistant, while his players include Harry Caesar (excellent), Pepper Martin, Ernie Wheelwright, Tony Cacciotti, Richard Kiel, Pervis Atkins, Sonny Sixkiller, Dino Washington and the imposing Bob Tessier. Lauter's beefcake brigade includes Mike Henry, Joe Knapp and Ray Nitschke. A mean bunch, believe it.

Besides debutante Ford, the largest female role is that of Bernadette Peters, playing Albert's horny secretary who, as she puts it, is "as far from Tallahassee as the prisoners." It's a cardboard, but catch-

ing, cameo role. Other good contributions come from John Steadman, a sage old lifer, also Mort Marshall as Albert's docile shadow, and Michael Fox, who calls the crucial game over the prison's own p.a. system.

The 121 minutes move along smartly, the final 47 minutes being the actual confrontations of the teams. The use of screen panels, a modish fad a few years ago but used in good context here, helps enliven and broaden audience interest in the game, while the Soul Touchers Band & Chorus provide good down-home cheering section musical emphasis. Frank De Vol's score is so unobtrusive as to seem nonexistent. A few other source song segments blend in well, and under the end titles there are a few bars of "Paramount on Parade," the old newsreel theme.

Joseph Biroc's lensing is tops, and production designer James S. Vance has well earned that premium credit. Michael Luciano's editing is trim, and football se-

168

Reynolds wears his favorite number—22—in The Longest Yard.

Burt's brother, Jim Reynolds, portrays Ice Man in The Longest Yard. *In real life, Jim coaches football at a high school in West Palm Beach, Florida.*

Burt Reynolds and Eddie Albert.

quence editing credits are given to Frank Capacchione, Allan Jacobs and George Hively. The climactic football play, the inspiration for the title, is played in excruciating but tantalizing super-slow motion, enough to bring an audience to its feet.

There is a major highlight when Reynolds and Albert have a showdown over throwing the game to the guards. The weakness of each man is played off against the other's in an exchange of superb acting, writing, and directorial artistry. This is one of Albert's finest screen performances.

As for Reynolds, it became obvious more than a year ago that he has reached merited stardom. Such an accomplishment always takes time, time during which the performer pulls together his various elements of charisma, and, on the audience end, the time not only to work into an acceptance of the player, but also to participate vicariously in his obvious growth. That's what made the "old" Hollywood star, and that's what's making the new ones of this era. Reynolds, along with Jack Nicholson, has paid his dues, and so have the audiences whose wait was not in vain.

Quarterback Paul Crewe.

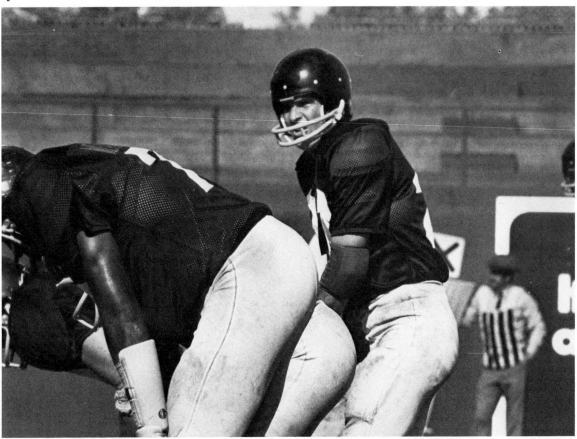

W.W. AND THE DIXIE DANCEKINGS

"It turned out wrong, but it made a lot of money. It was important that we didn't make fun of the people in Nashville. It was a bouquet to them."

—*B.R.*

CREDITS

(20th Century-Fox—1975)

Executive Producer, Steve Shagan; Producer, Stanley S. Canter; Director, John G. Avildsen; Screenwriter, Thomas Rickman; Cinematographer, Jim Crabe; Editor, Robbe Roberts; Production Designer, Larry Paull; Set Decorator, Jim Berkey; Music, David Grusin; Assistant Director, Ric Rondell; Special Effects, Milt Rice; Running Time, 94 minutes

CAST

W.W. Bright, Burt Reynolds; *Dixie,* Conny Van Dyke; *Wayne,* Jerry Reed; *Country Bull,* Ned Beatty; *Junior,* James Hampton; *Leroy,* Don Williams; *Butterball,* Richard Hurst; *Deacon Gore,* Art Carney; *Elton Bird,* Sherman G. Lloyd; *Good Ol' Boy Attendant,* Bill McCutcheon; *Golden Cowboy,* Mel Tillis; *Sourface (Attendant),* Fred Stuthman; *Uncle Furry,* Furry Lewis; *Hester Tate,* Mort Marshall; *June Ann,* Sherry Mathis; *Rosie,* Nancy Andrews; *Della,* Peg Murray; *Tootsie,* Herself

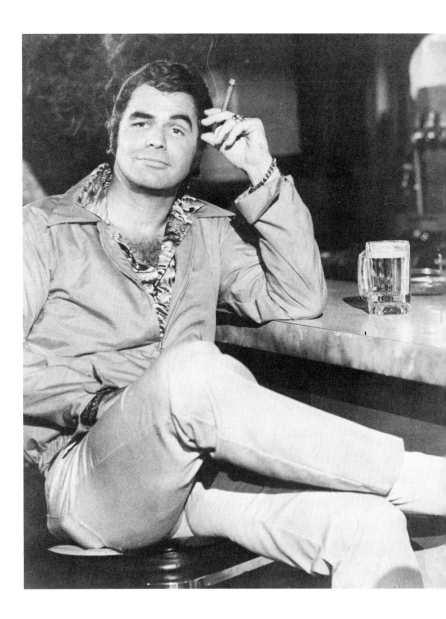

B.R. as W.W. Bright in W.W. and the Dixie Dancekings.

Left to right: *Richard Hurst, James Hampton, Don Williams, Conny Van Dyke, Jerry Reed, Burt Reynolds.*

PICK OF THE CRITICS
Kevin Thomas—*Los Angeles Times*—May 21, 1975

In *W.W. and the Dixie Dancekings* Burt Reynolds, as W.W., is a small-time con artist whose father taught him there are only two things that keep a man going in this world—himself and greed.

At least that's what W.W. tells a flabbergasted backwoods gas station operator who finds a pistol staring him in the face after his "customer" has laid on southern-fried geniality an inch thick.

Too smart to turn off the aw-shucks charm once he's pocketed the loot, he peels off a pair of hundreds and hands them to his astonished victim, explaining that it's not fair a man should be getting only $40 a week pay from an oil company hauling in $1 million a day. In return for his gen-

Burt Reynolds and Ned Beatty.

erosity, W.W. asks one small favor: tell the cops a bunch of rough-talking Yankees in a big Buick pulled the job.

But when a highway patrolman picks up the scent anyway, W.W. winds up jumping on to the stage of a humble dance hall and announcing a contest with a $25 prize. That saves his neck, at least for the moment, but more importantly it introduces him to baffled performers Dixie (Conny Van Dyke) and her Dancekings (Jerry Reed, James Hampton, Richard Hurst, Don Williams).

W.W. and the Dixie Dancekings, written by Thomas Rickman, not only is tailored perfectly for Reynolds but also is a very funny and surprisingly touching film. John Avildsen's direction is so carefully modu-

Burt Reynolds and Conny Van Dyke.

W.W. robs a gasoline station attendant named Sourface (Fred Stuthman).

lated, moving easily from the broadly humorous to the subtly serious, that he has been able to elicit a genuine emotional response to unabashed sentimentality. For *W.W. and the Dixie Danckings* is quite simply the very old story of the sharpie who intends to exploit some innocents but is instead melted by their goodness.

By now Reynolds is a master at portraying the self-mocking hustler, but the picture works so well because the winsome and talented Miss Van Dyke, a rising country and western singer in her screen debut, is so convincingly naive.

The progress of the Dixie Dancekings to Grand Ole Opry stardom is punctuated —i.e., the plot is furthered—by a running gag that has Art Carney as a delightfully dour fire-and brimstone fundamentalist preacher serving as a remorseless detective in pursuit of whoever it is who's knocking over all those gas stations owned by his fuddy-duddy pal (Sherman Lloyd), the president of that oil company with the $1 million daily income.

There are a couple of brief but crucial scenes with Ned Beatty playing a country star to subtly satirical perfection. Beatty's casual insulting of Miss Van Dyke followed by an abashed apology is a triumph of nuance that reveals much about the commercialized aspects of down-home music. Veteran guitar player Furry Lewis makes a touching screen debut as a kind of gentle godfather to Reed (in actuality a Nashville superstar).

Photographed entirely in Nashville and its environs, the film is highly atmospheric. Its rapid pacing is breezily punctuated by amusing old-fashioned cut-out wipes. Wisely, it has been set in 1957, not so much for purposes of nostalgia but simply because it would be mighty difficult to accept that anyone in the '70s could still be as innocent as Dixie and her Dancekings.

Burt Reynolds and Art Carney.

174

AT LONG LAST LOVE

"Not as bad a film as it was reviewed. I mean, nothing could be that bad. What was reviewed was Cybill Shepherd and Peter Bogdanovich's relationship. You see, Peter Bogdanovich has done something that all critics will never forgive him for doing. That is, stop being a critic, go make a film, and have that film **The Last Picture Show** *become enormously successful. Well, what he did then was go on talk shows and be rather arrogant and talk about how bad critics are. That was the final straw. So they were all waiting with their hatchets and knives and whatever. And along came Peter, who finally gave them something they could kill him with. Unfortunately, there I was, between Cybill's broad shoulders and Peter's ego. And I got buried along with them."*

—B.R.

CREDITS

(20th Century-Fox—1975)
Producer/Director/Screenwriter, Peter Bogdanovich; Associate Producer, Frank Marshall; Music & Lyrics, Cole Porter; Cinematographer, Laszlo Kovacs; Editor, Douglas Robertson; Production Designer, Gene Allen; Art Director, John Lloyd; Set Decorator, Jerry Wunderlich; Music Supervision, Artie Butler, Lionel Newman; Assistant Director, Mickey McArdle; Special Effects, Charlie Spurgeon; Running Time, 115 minutes

CAST

Michael Oliver Pritchard III, Burt Reynolds; *Brooke Carter,* Cybill Shepherd; *Kitty O'Kelly,* Madeline Kahn; *Johnny Spanish,* Duilio del Prete; *Elizabeth,* Eileen Brennan;

Mr. Reynolds as Michael Oliver Pritchard III in At Long Last Love.

Left to right: Cybill Shepherd, Madeline Kahn, Eileen Brennan, John Hillerman, Mildred Natwick, Duilio del Prete, Burt Reynolds.

Duilio del Prete slings a musical serving of roast beef while Madeline Kahn, Burt, and Cybill Shepherd give him their full attention.

Rodney James, John Hillerman; *Mabel Pritchard,* Mildred Natwick; *Doorman,* M. Emmet Walsh; *Cab Driver,* Artie Butler; *Telegram Bellboy,* Kevin O'Neal; *Bandleader,* Manny Harmon; *Salesgirl,* Anna Bogdanovich; *Children,* Antonia Bogdanovich, Alexandra Bogdanovich

PICK OF THE CRITICS
Roger Ebert—*Chicago Sun-Times*—March 25, 1975

It's impossible not to feel affection for *At Long Last Love,* Peter Bogdanovich's much-maligned evocation of the classical 1930s musical. It's light, silly, impeccably stylish entertainment, and if the performers don't come up to the comparisons they evoke with the genius of Astaire and Rogers, that's not entirely their fault; the studio tradition that developed and nurtured the great musical stars no longer exists, and a movie like this has to be made from scratch.

Well, not altogether from scratch. The music and lyrics are all by Cole Porter, a special enthusiasm of Bogdanovich and his star, Cybill Shepherd, who recorded an album of Porter last year. There are 16 Porter classics, and in an age when original songs composed for the movies tend to seek the level of "Love Theme from the Towering Inferno," maybe it's a good idea to go back to the golden age of popular American composition and cherish once again "It's De-Lovely," "Well, Did you Evah?," "Just One of Those Things" and the title song (which Porter actually began writing while waiting for the doctors to arrive at the scene of the accident that crippled him for life).

Bogdanovich has found a story and setting that sound the right tone in company with the songs. His screenplay involves a sophisticated (and yet sometimes childishly innocent) dalliance among four members of the idle rich or would-be rich (everyone's idle). There's Burt Reynolds as a playboy millionaire, Miss Shepherd as a beautiful heiress, Madeline Kahn as a Broadway star and Duilio del Prete as a seductive Latin gambler. They sip champagne almost without respite, dance the night away, run through a series of wrecked limousines and touring cars, trade partners and try never, ever, to be bored.

The story, of course, is totally inconsequential, as it should be, and Bogdanovich is good at keeping it floating some few inches above the ground; he's not giving us a tribute to the great musicals like "Swing Time" and "Top Hat," he's trying to make another one. He doesn't succeed, primarily because his performers aren't really suited to musical comedy, but he doesn't fail to the extent some of the reviews would have you believe.

Cybill Shepherd is a wonder to behold, but she isn't a gifted singer and no regimen of voice lessons is going to make her one. She didn't do a very good job on her Cole Porter album, and she's no better here, although at least we're permitted to see her as she sings, and that provides a certain compensation. Before Bogdanovich, a devoted student of movie classics, makes further attempts to present Miss Shepherd as a singer, he'd do well to rerun *Citizen Kane*, particularly the scene of Susan Alexander's disastrous opera debut.

Burt Reynolds, on the other hand, isn't really expected to sing and dance well. The fun is watching him try to have fun in a low-key way without making a fool of himself, and he generally succeeds. His Clark Gable–style moustache and his overall

Pritchard sings the title song while he shaves. It was Burt's idea to stick toilet tissue swatches over his shaving nicks in the scene—reminiscent of an occurrence in his own life when he nervously cut up his face before his first screen test.

The stars temporarily change partners.

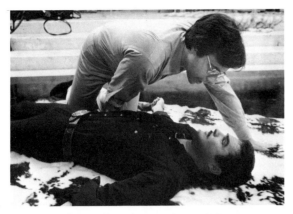

Director Peter Bogdanovich and Burt rehearse a scene in which Pritchard ends up on the floor after an exhausting musical routine.

bearing remind us of Gable grinning foolishly during absurd production numbers and having a ball. Miss Kahn is tart and has a nice edge, Del Prete is a satisfactory Latin lover and there's a very funny, understated supporting performance by John Hillerman as Rodney the butler.

The movie's no masterpiece, but I can't account for the viciousness of some of the critical attacks against it. It's almost as if Bogdanovich is being accused of the sin of pride for daring to make a musical to the classical Hollywood style. *At Long Last Love* isn't *Swing Time*, but it thankfully isn't *Funny Lady* either. Bogdanovich has too much taste, too sure a feel for the right tone, to go seriously wrong. And if he doesn't go spectacularly right, at least he provides small pleasures and great music.

Johnny Spanish, Kitty O'Kelly, Michael Pritchard, and Brooke Carter dance across the ballroom.

HUSTLE

"Catherine Deneuve and I were a case of one and one makes three, so that brought out some interest."

—*B.R.*

CREDITS
(Paramount—1975)
Producer/Director, Robert Aldrich; Associate Producer, William Aldrich; Screenwriter, Steve Shagan from his novel; Cinematographer, Joseph Biroc; Editor, Michael Luciano; Art Director, Hilyard Brown; Set Decorator, Raphael Bretton; Music, Frank De Vol; Assistant Director, Malcolm Harding; Special Effects, Henry Millar; Running Time, 120 minutes

CAST
Lieutenant Phil Gaines, Burt Reynolds; *Nicole*, Catherine Deneuve; *Marty Hollinger*, Ben Johnson; *Sergeant Belgrave*, Paul Winfield; *Paula Hollinger*, Eileen Brennan; *Leo Sellers*, Eddie Albert; *Santoro*, Ernest Borgnine; *Peggy Summers*, Catherine Bach; *Herbie Dalitz*, Jack Carter; *Gloria Hollinger*, Sharon Kelly; *Bus Driver*, James Hampton; *Bellamy*, David Spielberg; *Airport Bartender*, Donald "Red" Barry

Burt as Lieutenant Phil Gaines in Hustle.

The cop and the call girl.

Burt Reynolds and Catherine Deneuve.

Hustle aims for the gut.

Of course, that's the trademark of its director, Robert Aldrich. The man who made *The Dirty Dozen* and *Whatever Happened to Baby Jane?* has the considerable talent of winning audiences to his point of view by manipulating their emotions.

His last film, *The Longest Yard*, had audiences cheering—just as the ads claimed—while Burt Reynolds and his fellow convicts took on the prison guards in a brutal football game. Not even an avowed pacifist could fail to be exhilarated whenever "one of the bad guys" went down for the final count. The film bypassed the brain and got under your skin.

Hustle, however, is a much more complex film which forgoes characterizations in black and white. Much of the action of Aldrich's past films is absent here, but the result is a rewarding film that ends with two successive gut-grabbing scenes.

Burt Reynolds is Lieutenant Phil Gaines, a smug, hard-nosed Los Angeles police officer who understands the system and its limitations and works well within them—up to a point. Put in charge of investigating the death of a young girl whose body washes up on the beach, he decides there's really no need for anything more than a perfunctory investigation. After all, the coroner's report indicates she killed herself with an overdose of drugs, and who cares about the death of the daughter of a middle-class nobody?

Besides, Reynolds is grappling with woman trouble at the moment. The woman he may or may not love, Nicole, is a high-priced call girl. This bothers him, but he's at a loss about what to do. He's not ready for marriage, having only recently left his wife—after he discovered she was cheating on him.

But the dead girl's father (Ben Johnson) goads the police into investigating, insisting that his daughter was murdered. "Who's paying off the police?" he asks. "If I came in here with a high-priced lawyer things would be different, wouldn't they?"

Steve Shagan's screenplay is just fine, although a bit heavy handed in hammering out the theme that everyone is a hustler, equally willing to exploit others and sell themselves. "Sometimes you can't tell the

Christians from the lions," quips Reynolds.

But as Reynolds continues his investigation the script provides the opportunity for a notable cast—including Ernest Borgnine, Paul Winfield and Jack Carter—to sink their teeth into some good characters. Particularly outstanding are Ben Johnson and Eileen Brennan as the two anguished parents who know that the death of their daughter is really their fault, regardless of whether she was murdered or took her own life.

Reynolds, displaying once more his depth and versatility, is superb as a man wrestling with his conscience and emotions. He is particularly striking in the opening sequence, when he jokes with Catherine Deneuve about her calling. His enigmatic smile keeps the audience guessing: is he really so relaxed about his girlfriend being a prostitute, or is his kidding a defense

Hustle *was filmed in and around Los Angeles.*

Left to right: Ben Johnson, Paul Winfield, Burt Reynolds.

mechanism? Later developments justify Reynolds' ambiguous characterization.

As the film slowly builds, traditional concepts of right and wrong are slowly destroyed. Aldrich is saying that life is not so clean-cut, that all solutions are in reality imperfect. More important, Aldrich doesn't just state his message. He makes his audience feel it.

Lieutenant Gaines wipes off the telltale fingerprints after an angry citizen kills lawyer Leo Sellers (Eddie Albert).

Detective Reynolds shoots it out with psychotic killer David Spielberg.

LUCKY LADY

"I'm in the minority, mind you, but I don't think it was a bad film. I don't even think I turned in a bad performance."
—B.R.

CREDITS
(20th Century-Fox—1975)
Producer, Michael Gruskoff; Director, Stanley Donen; Screenwriters, Willard Huyck, Gloria Katz; Cinematographer, Geoffrey Unsworth; Editors, Peter Boita, George Hively; Production Designer, John Barry; Art Director, Norman Reynolds; Music, Ralph Burns; Assistant Director, Nigel Wooll; Running Time, 117 minutes

In Lucky Lady, *scrappy bootleggers Gene Hackman, Liza Minnelli, and Burt Reynolds become . . .*

. . . very affluent bootleggers.

CAST

Kibby, Gene Hackman; *Claire,* Liza Minnelli; *Walker,* Burt Reynolds; *Captain Masely,* Geoffrey Lewis; *McTeague,* John Hillerman; *Billy,* Robby Benson; *Captain Rockwell,* Michael Hordean; *Tully,* Anthony Holland; *Huggins,* John McLiam; *Dolf,* Val Avery; *Bernie,* Louis Guss; *Charley,* William H. Bassett; *Auctioneer,* Duncan McLeod; *Supercargo,* Milt (Lewis) Kogan; *Brunette,* Suzanne Zenor; *Redhead,* Majorie Battles

PICK OF THE CRITICS

Jay Cocks—*Time*—December 22, 1975

For the past year or so, the rallying cry for most American film producers has been "entertainment." Hollywood is interested almost entirely in showing audiences a good time, recycling traditional plots and characters, concentrating on star quality. What is most eagerly sought after is the glistening surface and full-throttle frivolity that characterized Hollywood films of the 1930s.

Luxurious, sassy and a lot of fun, *Lucky Lady* is very much a movie of the times—both now and then. It is a wise-cracking, softhearted romantic adventure in which the major characters seem modeled on movie stars. With the shade of Jean Harlow peering over her cocked shoulder, Liza Minnelli plays a '20s rumrunner called Claire Dobie. Gene Hackman and Burt Reynolds, her partners in crime, are like Tracy and Gable, fast friends and occasional antagonists, both in love with Claire. These three amorous buddies run booze up the California coast from Mexico, playing cat-and-mouse with the Coast Guard and doing battle with the mob boys who frown on independent action. They get rich and get shot at, sometimes all at once. This splendidly impossible sort of life is precarious and, as a consequence, exhilarating

The rambunctious sophistication of Stanley Donen's direction makes the amatory adventures whistle by as fast as the gunplay. Writers Huyck and Katz, who col- 185

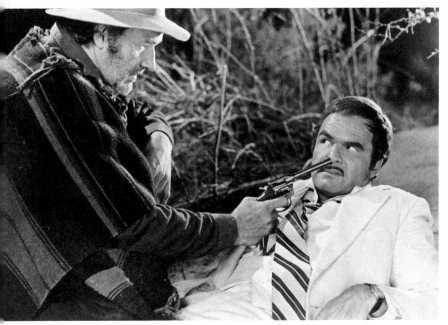

laborated with George Lucas on the screenplay for *American Graffiti,* are unashamedly infatuated with the myths and romances of old Hollywood but are shrewd enough not to mimic them. Their writing is affectionate, not slavish, and full of sly wit.

The three principals seem to realize their importance in maintaining the proper chemical balance. Liza Minnelli is better than she has ever been, sweet and raffish, while Burt Reynolds cuts up with infectious bemusement. Much of the heavy acting falls to Gene Hackman—just as it did to Spencer Tracy—and he performs with subdued authority. If the stars seem sometimes to be off on different courses, playing out their own roles instead of playing to

Kibby and Walker meet in an unfriendly manner before becoming allies.

Burt shouts battle directions during a comical sea fight.

Burt and cabin boy Robby Benson fight off rival bootleggers.

each other, this is one of the hazards of all-star Hollywood entertainment.

For all its breeziness, *Lucky Lady* falters over a few other hazards. The proceedings get a little arch at times: an occasional line seems too cherished, some secondary performances are rendered in strokes too broad. Besides, at the last minute the filmmakers changed the original ending, in which Hackman and Reynolds were killed, because preview audiences were disappointed. Now the three protagonists are last seen much older and still together. The happy ending is in one of Hollywood's best traditions. Those traditions can be limiting even when the show is flush with high spirits.

His ship lost, Burt keeps on paddling.

Walker and Kibby fear that their end is near.

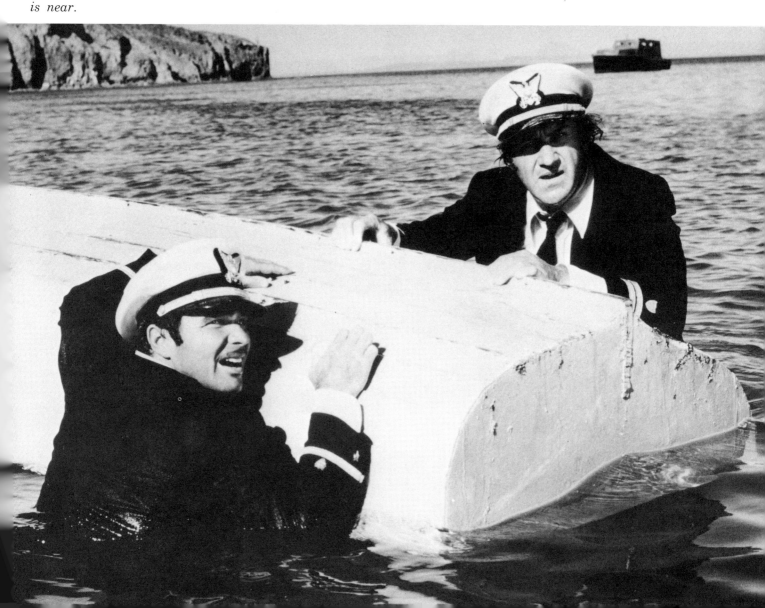

GATOR

"Gator was like Chinese food—not a great picture, but great entertainment, and you might want to go back for more a couple of hours later."

—B.R.

CREDITS
(United Artists—1976)
Producers, Jules Levy, Arthur Gardner; Director, Burt Reynolds; Screenwriter, William Norton; Cinematographer, William Fraker; Editor, Harold F. Kress; Art Director, Kirk Axtell; Music, Charles Bernstein; Assistant Director, Edward Teets; Special Effects, Cliff Wenger; Technical Adviser, Jerry Imber; Running Time, 115 minutes

CAST
Gator McKlusky, Burt Reynolds; *Irving Greenfield,* Jack Weston; *Aggie Maybank,* Lauren Hutton; *Bama McCall,* Jerry Reed; *Emmeline Cavanaugh,* Alice Ghostley; *Mayor Caffrey,* Dub Taylor; *Governor,* Mike Douglas; *Smiley,* Burton Gilliam; *Bones,* William Engesser; *Ned McKlusky,* John Steadman; *Suzie McKlusky,* Lori Futch; *Teenage Addict,* Stephanie Burchfield; *Man in Hospital,* Bob Yeager; *Pogie,* Dudley Remus; *Police Chief,* Alex Hawkins

PICK OF THE CRITICS
Jerry Renninger—*Palm Beach Post*—July 23, 1976

   Gator is a wild, entertaining movie, and it's not necessary to have been weaned on grits and sour mash to enjoy it.
   Burt Reynolds resurrects Gator McKlusky, the character he created for *White Lightning,* to help the good guys stop the bad guys once again, albeit unwillingly. By threatening to throw his daddy in jail for moonshining, the federals

Burt Reynolds and Lauren Hutton in Gator.

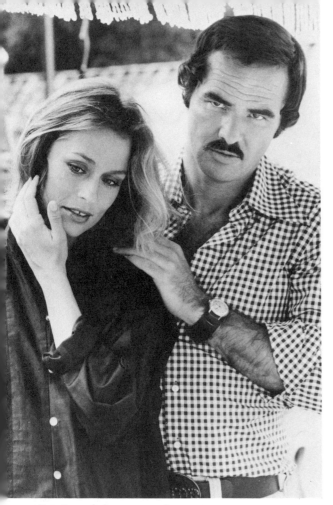

Burt and Lauren rehearse a scene.

Burt sets up a courtroom scene. Seated at the right, wearing horn-rimmed glasses, is professor Watson B. Duncan III. Dr. Duncan steered college student Buddy Reynolds towards an acting career.

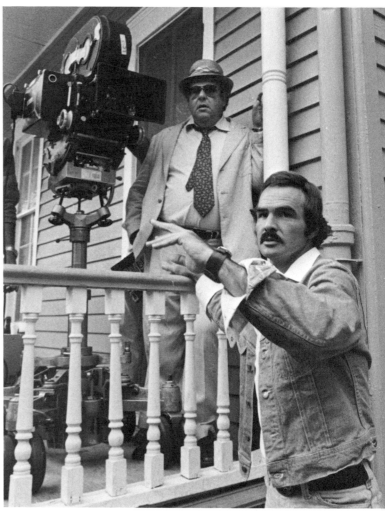

Director Reynolds discusses an outdoor sequence with Jack Weston.

TV host Mike Douglas, portraying a governor in Gator, *poses with the director.*

force Gator to help them nail an old school buddy named Bama McCall (Jerry Reed), now a corrupt political boss.

As if that weren't enough, he has to deal with the likes of an incompetent agent (Jack Weston), a nosy TV reporter (Lauren Hutton) and a deranged City Hall clerk (Alice Ghostley). Out of the boat chases, car chases and generalized mayhem emerges a well-acted, well-directed and surprisingly funny film.

There's nothing spectacular about the actual story, and the characters (on paper) are relatively conventional. What keeps *Gator* out of the swamps is unconventional acting by all hands and remarkably good direction by Reynolds. This is the first film he has directed, but it's plain that his many years as an actor have taught him how the job should be done.

Most of the movie's humor is the direct result of fine character acting rather than clever dialogue. At this Jack Weston is particularly gifted. Few actors have his knack for drawing laughter from anguish, both physical and mental. He suffers so well and so graphically that it's not possible to remain calm in the face of it. Alice Ghostley, on the other hand, transforms herself into a harmless harpy who must be suffered herself.

For the first time in her acting career, Lauren Hutton gives evidence that she indeed can act. This isn't to say she never knew how, but before *Gator,* all her roles seemed to consist of taking up space in front of the camera.

The real surprise comes from Jerry Reed. In the second film role of his career, this Nashville composer and singer comes off as one of the most genial and interesting villains you've ever seen. He puts on his best Amos Moses accent, swaggers around like a drugstore cowboy, and turns in a perfectly

190

Underworld baddie Bama McCall gets
beaten up by good ol' boy Gator
McKlusky.

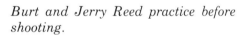

Burt and Jerry Reed practice before
shooting.

Burt flees from the State Revenue Department's helicopter in a high-powered speedboat.

Burt continues his getaway. It ends when his boat cuts through and completely demolishes a river shack. A double performed the portion involving the structure.

beastly performance. He may never play Hamlet, but then the world is full of Hamlets.

If anything, Burt Reynolds' acting seems more enhanced than marred by his own direction. He employs more subtlety than the role really demands, and his manner is more subdued than you'd expect in a moonshining swamp rat. Yet the overall effect is pleasing. It's as if he had a clearer vision of Gator's position in relation to the other characters because of his unique viewpoint, namely from the director's chair. Many actors who have attempted to direct themselves fall down both as actors and directors. Happily that's far from being the case here.

Gator was designed and executed as an entertainment, and it has no apologies to make in this regard. Too often "entertainment" is a defensive euphemism intended to justify stupidity, crudity and sloppiness. None of those conditions exist here. It's just fun to watch.

SILENT MOVIE

"I had this big house up on a hill. I had gotten a big 'R' from Republic Studios and put it on the gate. The decor was Early Gauche. I had my initials everywhere— 'BR' on the rugs, the ashtrays, everything. I used to put lights around the 'R' for parties. It made me laugh. It's the kind of joke I like to play on myself. Mel Brooks took that real-life joke and ran with it for the part I played in Silent Movie."

—B.R.

In Silent Movie, *Marty Feldman, Dom De Luise, and Mel Brooks sneak up on Burt as he takes a shower.*

*The big 'R' on Burt's front gate—
inspiration for Mel Brooks.*

CREDITS
(20th Century-Fox—1976)
Producer, Michael Hertzberg; Director, Mel Brooks; Screenwriters, Mel Brooks, Ron Clark, Rudy De Luca, Barry Levinson from a story by Ron Clark; Cinematographer, Paul Lohman; Editors, John C. Howard, Stanford C. Allen; Production Designer, Al Brenner; Set Decorator, Rick Simpson; Music, John Morris; Assistant Director, Edward Teets; Special Effects, Ira Anderson, Jr.; Running Time, 86 minutes

CAST
Mel Funn, Mel Brooks; *Marty Eggs*, Marty Feldman; *Dom Bell*, Dom De Luise; *Vilma Kaplan*, Bernadette Peters; *Studio Chief*, Sid Caesar; *Engulf*, Harold Gould; *Devour*, Ron Carey; *Pregnant Lady*, Carol Arthur; *Newspaper Vendor*, Liam Dunn; *Maitre d'*, Fritz Feld; *Studio Gate Guard*, Chuck McCann; *Nurse*, Valerie Curtin; *Studio Chief's Secretary*, Yvonne Wilder; *Acupuncture Man*, Arnold Soboloff; *Motel Bellhop*, Patrick Campbell; *Man in Tailor Shop*, Harry Ritz; *Blind Man*, Charlie Callas; *Fly-in-Soup Man*, Henny Youngman; *British Officer*, Eddie Ryder; *Anne Bancroft*, Herself; *James Caan*, Himself; *Marcel Marceau*, Himself; *Liza Minnelli*, Herself; *Paul Newman*, Himself; *Burt Reynolds*, Himself

PICK OF THE CRITICS
Gene Shalit—*Ladies' Home Journal*—September 1976

Mel Brooks, who made *The Producers*, plus *Blazing Saddles* and *Young Frankenstein*, has now made *Silent Movie*, which *is*

Burt Reynolds and Mel Brooks.

silent, except for the background music, the sound effects and the uproarious laughter from the audience. Mel plays Mel Funn, a Hollywood director downed by drink, who craves to carve a comeback by making a silent movie. His sidekicks are Marty Feldman (with the bulging eyes) and Dom De Luise (with the bulging belly). They set out to persuade top Hollywood stars to participate. I won't give away these guest stars, but I will say that *one* is Burt Reynolds, who proves what I have been saying for years: that given the right roles, he could be the most sophisticated Cary Grant–like comedian on the screen today,

and could dump all of that macho muck. Brooks has provided *Silent Movie* with printed titles that are simply understated and simply hilarious. Arthur Schnabel, the great pianist, once said that Mozart wrote music with a small quantity of notes which produced a great quality of music. In *Silent Movie,* there is small quantity (a certain purity infuses the screen) and the result is great quality. I may not be making myself clear, but I know what I mean. The fact is that this is a film for everyone: it is a comedy treasure, and Mel Brooks and *Silent Movie* are too funny for words.

Burt, Dom, and Mel.

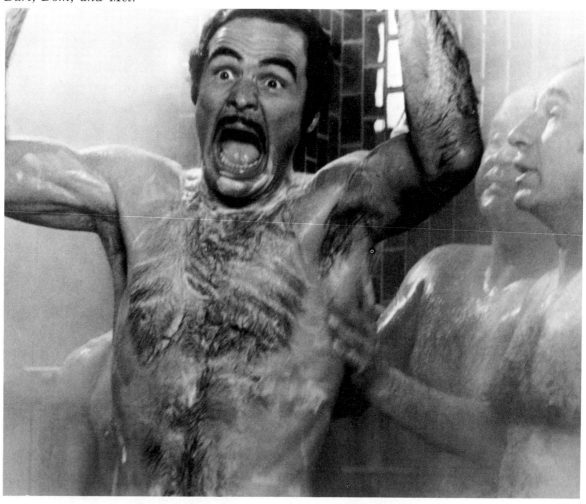

NICKELODEON

"I didn't have any fun on Nickelodeon. I was ill. It showed."

—B.R.

CREDITS
(Columbia—1976)
Producers, Irwin Winkler, Robert Chartoff; Associate Producer, Frank Marshall; Director, Peter Bogdanovich; Screenwriters, W.D. Richter, Peter Bogdanovich; Cinematographer, Laszlo Kovacs; Editor, William Carruth; Art Director, Richard Berger; Set Decorator, Darrell Silvera; Music, Richard Hazard; Assistant Director, Jack Sanders; Special Effects, Cliff Wenger; Running Time, 121 minutes

CAST
Leo Harrigan, Ryan O'Neal; *Buck Greenway,* Burt Reynolds; *Alice Forsyth,* Tatum O'Neal; *H.H. Cobb,* Brian Keith; *Marty Reeves,* Stella Stevens; *Franklin Frank,* John Ritter; *Kathleen Cooke,* Jane Hitchcock; *Mabel,* Priscilla Pointer; *Waldo,* Don Calfa; *Hecky,* Mathew Anden; *Harry,* James Best; *Pete,* Harry Carey, Jr.; *Father Logan,* M. Emmet Walsh

PICK OF THE CRITICS
Kathleen Carroll—New York *Daily News*—December 22, 1976

As a dedicated film historian with a passionate attachment for old movies, director Peter Bogdanovich has plainly poured his all into the making of *Nickelodeon.* The

Burt as Buck Greenway in Nickelodeon.

film is his own sentimental toast to the movie industry—an exuberant reminder of the days when movies were just a novel form of entertainment costing all of five cents.

As *Nickelodeon* tells it, moviemaking was a pretty haphazard process when the industry was in its infancy. The patent office had declared war on the independent producers, and they were scrambling for survival. Stars were born more out of endurance and necessity than out of good looks and talent. Scripts were casually concocted on the spot, and all one had to do to become a director was to look authoritative and yell "cut!" on cue.

In attempting to recapture the lunatic spirit of this kind of catch-as-catch-can moviemaking, Bogdanovich has turned

Burt Reynolds and Jane Hitchcock.

Buck douses Leo Harrigan (Ryan O'Neal) with champagne punch.

Nickelodeon into a rollicking farce, a frantic free-for-all packed with hilariously old-fashioned slapstick. Then, towards the end of the film, there is a sharp, rather disconcerting shift in mood: actors stop their frolicking, and the characters they're playing suddenly begin to appear more human and vulnerable.

Bogdanovich himself adopts a more serious, reflective tone to show that, with the end of the nickelodeon era and the emergence of Hollywood as a movie Mecca, the screen had lost a certain innocence. Beneath its giddy surface, *Nickelodeon* is a subtly detailed history of the movie business—from its rowdy beginnings to its artistic birth via the release of D.W. Griffith's *The Birth of a Nation*.

As the film's major stars, Ryan O'Neal

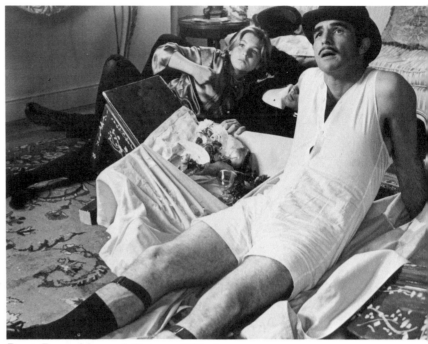

Burt Reynolds and Tatum O'Neal.

Burt and Ryan dry off after the champagne-throwing scene.

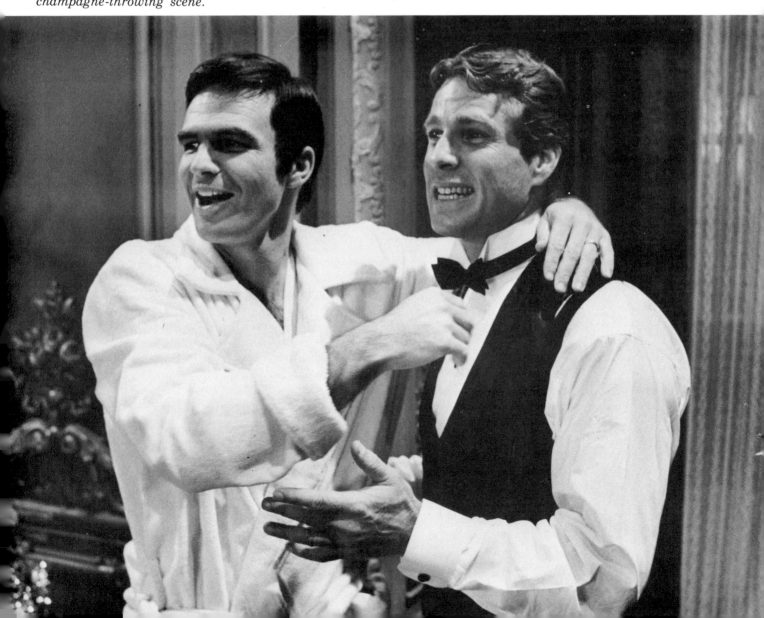

and Burt Reynolds have rarely been more appealing. O'Neal proves to be quite adept at this kind of knockabout, physical comedy (as he did in Bogdanovich's *What's Up, Doc?*), and Reynolds shelves the sarcasm and acts the role of a country bumpkin who stumbles into the leading man league and grows disillusioned with the silly demands that go with the job. Tatum O'Neal adds her perky charm to a relatively minor role, while Jane Hitchcock has the appropriately fragile look of a silent screen heroine.

Nickelodeon does not always work, but it can completely entrance anyone who shares Bogdanovich's intense fascination with the bright lights, the cameras and the whole magical process of moviemaking.

Stella Stevens, director Peter Bogdanovich, John Ritter, and Burt share a light moment in between takes.

Six Nickelodeon *members (among them James Best and Tatum O'Neal on the ground) restrain Burt when he is challenged by Ryan O'Neal and Harry Carey, Jr.*

Up, up, and away ... a hot-air balloon stunt.

SMOKEY AND THE BANDIT

"I've seen Smokey many times, and each time it makes me smile. Perhaps that's the simple secret of its success."

—B.R.

CREDITS

(Universal—1977)
Executive Producer, Robert L. Levy; Producer, Mort Engelberg; Director, Hal Needham; Screenwriters, James Lee Barrett, Charles Shyer, Alan Mandel from a story by Hal Needham and Robert L. Levy; Cinematographer, Bobby Byrne; Editor, Walter Hanneman; Art Director, Mark

Burt Reynolds as Bandit.

Sally Field as Frog.

Mansbridge; Set Decorator, Tony Montenaro; Music, Bill Justis, Jerry Reed; Assistant Director, David Hamburger; Special Effects, Art Brewer; Running Time, 97 minutes

CAST
Bandit, Burt Reynolds; *Carrie (Frog)*, Sally Field; *Sheriff Buford T. Justice (Smokey)*, Jackie Gleason; *Cledus (Snowman)*, Jerry Reed; *Junior*, Mike Henry; *Little Enos*, Paul Williams; *Big Enos*, Pat McCormick; *Traffic Patrolman*, Alfie Wise; *Branford*, George Reynolds; *Mr. B.*, Macon McCalman; *Waynette*, Linda McClure; *Hot Pants*, Susan McIver; *Branford's Deputy*, Michael Mann; *Sugar Bear*, Lamar Jackson, *Georgia Trooper*, Ronnie Gay; *Alabama Trooper*, Quinnon Sheffield

PICK OF THE CRITICS
Gary Arnold—*The Washington Post*—July 29, 1977

Smokey and the Bandit is an unexpected good time, a playful, wisecracking and curiously revealing example of All-American escapist entertainment.

In this instance the escapist appeal has been transparently yet ingeniously custom-built into the plot, which deals with a high-speed automotive chase from Texarkana to Atlanta and suggests nothing so much as a feature-length, live-action adaptation of a Roadrunner cartoon.

Burt Reynolds, relaxed and debonair beneath a cowboy hat and behind the wheel of a black Pontiac Trans Am, stars in the Roadrunner role, pursued by Jackie Gleason as an increasingly choleric Wile E. Coyote in lawman's clothing. We're never asked to accept the pretext for the chase as anything but a joke, yet the film is skillful and energetic enough to keep breezing along on the flimsiest of pretexts. In the long run it seems a fresh stylistic triumph: the first consistent, sustained screwball comedy about macho good ol' boys on the open road.

Reynolds' character, nicknamed Bandit, is a carefree, contemporary saddle tramp encountered at the Georgia State Finals of the Truck Roadeo, a drag-racing competition for truckers. A rich, self-indulgent, gambling Texan, Big Enos, and his diminutive son Little Enos—a hereditary monstrosity embodied by Pat McCormick and Paul Williams in matching outfits—approach the napping Bandit with an offer of $80,000 for bringing back a shipment of confiscated Coors from Texarkana within 28 hours. As Big Enos explains this whim, "I've got a boy runnin' in this Southern classic and when he wins, I want to celebrate in style!"

Bandit wakes up laughing at these undeniably funny-looking big shots and can't re-

Jackie Gleason as Smokey.

sist commenting on their wardrobe: "It must have been a bitch finding those suits in a 68 fat and a 12 dwarf." Naturally, he can't resist their offer, either. Bandit engages his best pal, trucker and family man Cledus (Jerry Reed), to drive his 18-wheel rig while he runs interference in the Trans Am.

The trip to Texarkana is quick and uneventful. The complications begin on the return trip, when Bandit picks up a runaway bride—Sally Field is a chorine named Carrie who got stranded and desperate during her first Southern tour. Carrie's jilted prospective father-in-law is the Gleason character, a Texas sheriff named Buford T. Justice.

Like McCormick's Big Enos, Gleason's Buford is accompanied by an impossible offspring—Mike Henry as a brawny dumbbell called Junior, whose main function turns out to be holding his daddy's hat on after the top of their car is sheared off. Like Big Enos, Buford also acts out of whimsically self-centered motives; he is determined to bring Carrie back because "Nobody walks out on a pretty weddin' I set up."

There have been a number of live-action films with the kind of comic consistency one associates with cartoons: the Inspector Clouseau vehicles and the Bond adventure *Live and Let Die* come immediately to mind. *Smokey and the Bandit* does something a little more: it combines cartoon stylization with screwball comedy stylization, producing a kind of supercharged comedy of manners that exploits down-home, regional, working-class American stereotypes.

The characters in *Smokey* are as exaggerated and ritualized as the characters in such '30s movies as *My Man Godfrey*, *Bringing Up Baby* or *You Can't Take It with You*. They inhabit a streamlined, farcical universe that rarely seems to impinge on reality, and then speak in a jaunty, hyperbolic idiom, liberally seasoned with Southern slang, CB slang and profanity, that seems an equally exotic and funny stylization of the language.

Millionaire father Pat McCormick and look-alike son Paul Williams offer fast-movin' Bandit a deal he can't refuse.

Burt and Jerry Reed with a basset hound called Fred in the script. The dog, tagged Happy by his owners, won the movie role via a "canine beauty pageant" held in Atlanta.

It's a considerable achievement to sustain such an illusion. I haven't the slightest idea which of the credited writers—James Lee Barrett, Charles Shyer or Alan Mandel—may be responsible for perfecting the idiom, assuming any of them did. On the other hand, Hal Needham appears to deserve credit for an exceptionally adept and good-humored directing debut following a 20-year career as a stunt man and stunt supervisor, most recently in vehicles starring his good friend Burt Reynolds.

One might have anticipated good stunt scenes, and there are several amusing chase and crash sequences in *Smokey*, but Needham seems to possess a comic outlook and timing extending beyond his erstwhile specialty. The prevailing mood of the film is cheerful and witty. Every element seems to be in balance, from the flirtatious exchange of Reynolds and Field, who make an endearing romantic comedy team, to throwaway bits of business, like the moment when Field begins practicing a dance step on the inside of the Trans Am windshield.

Needham also demonstrates a form of comic-poetic rabble-rousing talent that reminds one of Frank Capra at his most affectionate and, thankfully, least mawkish. Bandit's freewheeling form of banditry is linked directly to a distinctively American love of cars and the feeling of freedom that cars can bring. On the return trip Bandit is assisted by a brotherhood of CBers that crosses sexual, racial and even international lines.

Although it opened to indifferent reviews and business in New York two months ago, *Smokey and the Bandit* has already grossed close to $25 million in the South and Southwest. It will probably turn out to be one of the year's most popular and profitable films, and the potential appeal should have been obvious, even from New York.

It might not be a bad idea if the Carter administration also took a look, because this film is in touch with certain deepfelt national preferences. *Smokey and the Bandit* seems both an authentic and exuberant expression of how much taking the wheel means to Americans.

Burt, Sally, and Jerry relax before changing clothes for the next Smokey and the Bandit *scene.*

Burt checks out a camera angle while director Hal Needham (second from right) and cinematographer Bobby Byrne (extreme right) take back seats.

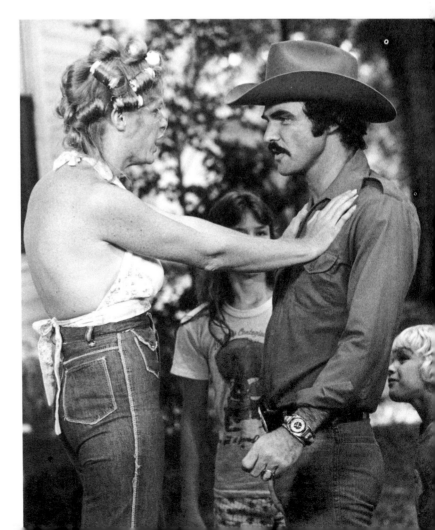

Burt Reynolds and supporting player Linda McClure.

SEMI-TOUGH

"I patterned Billy Clyde after Don Meredith. We filmed some scenes giving more background on Billy and his relationship with other players on the team, but for some reason those scenes were cut out."

—B.R.

CREDITS
(United Artists—1977)
Producer, David Merrick; Director, Michael Ritchie; Screenwriter, Walter Bernstein based on the novel by Dan Jenkins; Cinematographer, Charles Rosher, Jr.; Editor, Richard A. Harris; Production Designer, Walter Scott Herndon; Set Decorator, Cheryal Kearney; Music, Jerry Fielding; Assistant Director, Ken Swor; Running Time, 107 minutes

CAST
Billy Clyde Puckett, Burt Reynolds; *Shake Tiller*, Kris Kristofferson; *Barbara Jane Bookman*, Jill Clayburgh; *Big Ed Bookman*, Robert Preston; *Friedrich Bismark*, Bert Convy; *Puddin*, Roger E. Mosley; *Clara Pelf*, Lotte Lenya; *Phillip Hooper*, Richard Masur; *Dreamer Tatum*, Carl Weathers; *T.J. Lambert*, Brian Dennehy; *Earlene*, Mary Jo Catlett; *Hose Manning*, Joe Kapp; *Vlada*, Ron Silver; *McNair*, Jim McKrell; *Interpreter*, Peter Bromilow; *Coach Parks*, Norm Alden; *Minister*, Fred Stuthman; *Dressmaker*, Janet Brandt; *Fitter*, William Wolf; *Stewardess*, Jenifer Shaw; *Puddin, Jr.*, Kevin Furry; *Puddin's Wife*, Ava Roberts

PICK OF THE CRITICS
Richard Schickel—*Time*—November 21, 1977

Semi-Tough may or may not turn out to be the year's best comedy—there's *Annie Hall* to remember and Mel Brooks yet to be heard from—but it is without a doubt the year's most socially useful film. Dan Jenkins' best-seller has been slow to reach the screen, and in the intervening years the subject of his satire—pro football's Lombardi era, with all its dark Nixonian overtones—has lost some of its edge. Adapter Walter Bernstein and director Michael Ritchie have found a contemporary lunacy with the same rich possibilities in the human-potential movement, and for that they earn the gratitude of right thinkers everywhere. The Kilgore Rangerettes really ought to spell out their names between halves of the Super Bowl.

Jenkins' good ol' boy heroes are just the

Semi-Tough threesome—Kris Kristofferson, Jill Clayburgh, and Burt Reynolds.

Burt as Billy Clyde Puckett and Kris as Shake Tiller.

Burt Reynolds and Robert Preston.

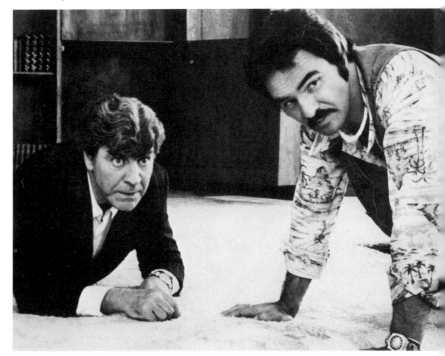

same. Billy Clyde Puckett (Burt Reynolds) is still a nately shrewd running back with a gift for putting on people who think they're smarter than he is because they don't talk in a Southern Conference drawl. His roommate and lifelong good buddy, Shake Tiller (Kris Kristofferson), is still a sticky-fingered end and an ernest naif. They are still involved, more as pals than lovers (though that, in time, develops) with Barbara Jane Bookman (Jill Clayburgh). She is a version of that most delicious of Hemingway's conceits—the intelligent and entirely feminine woman who is capable of being a man's man when the occasion warrants it.

What disturbs the good-natured serenity of this trio now is not the spartan demands and hope of playing in the Super

Left to right: Jill Clayburgh, Burt Reynolds, Kris Kristofferson.

Lotte Lenya portrays a stern physical therapist who administers brutal treatment to jock clients.

Bowl but the intrusion of self-realization. There is a special emphasis on an est-like movement called BEAT. Shake is converted to it, and his new-found saintliness threatens the stability of the *maison à trois*. His "seriousness" turns Barbara Jane's head. She must be rescued from both BEAT and marriage by Reynolds, who pretends a conversion of his own in order to expose the shallowness of the movement. The Ritchie-Bernstein version of an est seminar is done with marvelous malice, but it is not their only target. Along the way they take on rolfing, pyramid power and even something called movagenics, which invites its adepts to drop down on all fours and crawl around looking for their lost center of consciousness as if it were a cuff link that had rolled under the bed. Indeed, the mov-

Billy Clyde celebrates victory with two unidentified cheerleaders.

ie's funniest moment occurs when Robert Preston, a Texas oilman who owns the team, attempts to proselytize for this cult. He has had an office built to facilitate practice of his new faith. It has a teeny-tiny door you can enter only on your knees, a legless desk resting on the rug, pictures hung at baseboard level.

What that scene says is that no one—not even the semi-tough-minded among us—is immune to the absurdities of ideologies that hold out a promise of instant salvation. On a slightly deeper level, the movie is warning us to beware celebrities bearing false prophecies. Because of the absorption in self and craft that their work requires, performers—be they actors or athletes—can be easy converts, and therefore untrustworthy in their wayward enthusiasms for abstract realms. On the more positive side,

the picture suggests that if salvation is to be had, it lies in that pragmatic resistance to the con that has traditionally characterized the American spirit and is so charmingly exemplified by Reynolds.

All the leading players are nice to hang out with, though Clayburgh, who blends something of Carole Lombard and Jean Arthur, deserves special mention. The script talks R-rough, but there is a sweetness as well as smartness in it. The acute observation of cult behavior, not to mention the sporting life, suggests painful research somewhere along the way. The picture is, above all, a principled comedy, speaking lightly but honestly about life as it is—and what it might be—in our times. That sets *Semi-Tough* apart from anything else in recent memory.

Burt gets the girl.

THE END

"I asked other directors for advice. Bob Aldrich told me to always listen to everybody, and Mel Brooks told me to remember to fire someone the first day."
—B.R.

CREDITS
(Paramount—1978)
Executive Producer, Hank Moonjean; Producer, Lawrence Gordon; Associate Producer, James Best; Director, Burt Reynolds; Screenwriter, Jerry Belson; Cinematographer, Bobby Byrne; Editor, Donn Cambern; Production Designer, Jan Scott; Set Decora-

Death is a laughing matter for Burt Reynolds and Dom De Luise in The End.

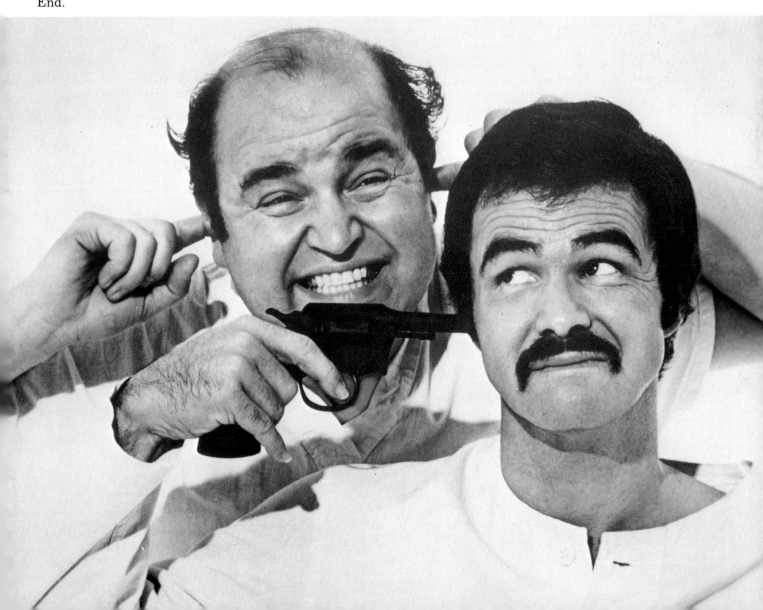

Terminally ill Sonny Lawson (Burt) threatens suicide, but Mary Ellen (Sally Field) knows the gun isn't loaded.

tor, John Franco, Jr.; Music, Paul Williams; Assistant Director, Kurt Baker; Special Effects, Cliff Wenger, Carol Wenger; Technical Adviser, Dorothy Vitale; Running Time, 99 minutes

CAST

Sonny Lawson, Burt Reynolds; *Marlon Borunki*, Dom De Luise; *Mary Ellen*, Sally Field; *Dr. Kling*, Strother Martin; *Marty Lieberman*, David Steinberg; *Jessica*, Joanne Woodward; *Dr. Krugman*, Norman Fell; *Maureen Lawson*, Myrna Loy; *Julie Lawson*, Kristy McNichol; *Ben Lawson*, Pat O'Brien; *The Priest*, Robby Benson; *Dr. Maneet*, Carl Reiner; *Receptionist*, Louise Letourneau; *Hearse Driver*, Bill Ewing; *Limousine Driver*, Robert Rothwell; *Hospital Orderly*, Harry Caesar; *Pacemaker Patient*, James Best; *Latin Lover*, Peter Gonzales;

Girl Dancer, Connie Fleming; *Ballet Teacher*, Janice Carroll; *Whistling Lunatic*, Ken Johnson; *Tall Male Nurse*, Frank McRae; *Short Male Nurse*, Alfie Wise; *Insurance Man*, Edward Albrecht; *Gardener*, Jerry Fujikawa; *Old Man*, Jock Mahoney; *Old Man's Son*, Patrick Moody; *Old Man's Daughter-in-Law*, Carolyn Martin; *Old Lady in Car*, Queenie Smith; *Driving Teacher*, Jean Ann Coulter

PICK OF THE CRITICS

John Barbour—*Los Angeles Magazine*—June 1978

During the past few weeks, Burt Reynolds has made more TV appearances that Mrs. Olson. Half the time he's been selling a movie called *The End*. The other half he's been telling critics they can kiss it. In much the same way Nixon keeps protesting his innocence, Reynolds keeps protesting to Merv and Mike and Dinah and Johnny that critics don't mean anything. On one of these shows, he said that he has never lied to the public about what to expect from films like *White Ligntning*, *Gator* and *Semi-Tough*. Why then should he expect critics to?

If I were Reynolds and I had made *Smokey and the Bandit*, which was little more than a Roadrunner cartoon, I wouldn't listen to what the critics had to say, either. I'd listen to my accountant. As an old Spanish proverb, and an Italian singer from Hoboken, say: "The good life is the best revenge!"

If Reynolds is looking for the good life and revenge, he will get both from *The End*. And if he's looking to dump on critics he'd better get it out of his system *now*, because after all the reviews are in he won't have them to kick around anymore. Because there won't be that many who won't love the film.

The End is the best thing Reynolds has ever done, either as an actor or a director. There are some individual scenes in it, written by Jerry Belson, that are as bright and sharp and funny as those of any comedy to come out of Hollywood since Reynolds told Darren McGavin where he could shove *Riverboat*.

Our star plays a TV real-estate salesman who is told that God is about to foreclose on him. Over the opening credits we hear him talking to a nurse who is preparing him for a urinalysis. It's like a good radio show, and the audience starts to giggle. It's a perfect setup for the movie—and for Reynolds' first line on camera. When we finally see him he is standing forlornly in the doctor's office. He says, "I have the same thing Ali McGraw had in *Love Story*."

He goes on to tell the doctor he didn't know he was sick, he just thought he'd found a new way of losing weight: throwing up. When he leaves the doctor's office, depressed, the first thing he sees is a funeral cortege, which he follows to the graveyard; and as he sits in his car contemplating his future, we see the shadow of the crucifix on the church steeple outlined on his forehead. It's a terrific touch.

Myrna Loy and Pat O'Brien as Burt's parents.

Mary Ellen's housekeeping leaves something to be desired.

Kristy McNichol as Burt's teen-age daughter.

Committed to an asylum, Sonny is visited by attorney David Steinberg and ex-wife Joanne Woodward.

Reynolds then goes to a young priest (played by Robby Benson) to confess for the first time in twenty years. The confrontation between him and Benson is a classic of underplayed comedy—so good it is almost British. Reynolds feels that Benson is a little too young to be called "Father"; Benson tells him he can call him "Dave." So Reynolds begins his confession with, "Forgive me, Dave, for I have sinned."

Following a bungled suicide attempt, Reynolds is committed to an asylum. Here he encourages a fellow inmate to try to kill him. The inmate, played by Dom De Luise, is a Polish psycho who strangled his father for tormenting him with Polish jokes; his monologue, in which he blurts out examples of these dreadful jokes to a bedridden Reynolds while sobbing over his father's fate, is magnificent. It's the kind of performance that elicits applause from an audience and Oscars from the Academy.

Because so much in *The End* is so good,

Left to right: Burt Reynolds, Myrna
Loy, Joanne Woodward.

the flaws can be forgiven. In the second
half De Luise's presence seems to over-
whelm Reynolds', and from here on the
film at times takes on a frantic, slapstick
broadness that had earlier been avoided.

Reynolds and author Belson also set us
up for what could have been a great
moment—one which the audience is led to
expect but which never takes place. Carl
Reiner, as a terminally ill psychiatrist
counseling the patients in the institution,
invites Reynolds to participate in an encounter group of others who are also about
to die. At this point we anticipate the kind
of deliciously dark humor and characters
possible in such a scene. When we don't
see it, we miss it.

At the end of The End Reynolds swims
out into the Pacific to drown, to the accom-
paniment of Frank Sinatra singing "My
Way." When he decides that he really
wants to live, even for a few months, he
screams out a wonderfully written soliloquy
to God for help that touches the heart and
funny bone. He tells God that if He helps
him get to shore, he'll give Him fifty percent of the gross—but the closer he gets to
shore the smaller God's share becomes.
Well, once a real-estate salesman, always a
real-estate salesman.

There was a time when Hollywood was
peopled by performers like Cary Grant,
William Powell, Spencer Tracy, Jimmy
Stewart and a handful of other consummate craftsmen and professionals who could
move from drama to comedy and back
again as easily as a turn of the page of a

script. They were talents and personalities;
often it was difficult to tell where one
stopped and the other began. They pos-
sessed the kind of versatility that today's
filmmaking no longer encourages—or re-
wards.

Today there are a handful of actors from
the New York school of realism heralded
for the genius with which they spit and
scratch. In drama some of them are brilliant, but in comedy they make the audience want to spit and scratch. Many give
the impression they aren't in acting for a
profession but for analysis. And perhaps
they've developed their considerable talents
for offbeat characterizations because they
have no personality. The farther away they
get from themselves, the better they perform.

Burt Reynolds, on the other hand, seems
to be a performer who likes himself. And
for good reason. He's a survivor in an industry and a country where individuality is
on the endangered-species list. In films, his
problem has been that his own personality
was much more interesting and appealing
than most of the parts he played. For him,
though—to paraphrase that terrible commercial for the Los Angeles Times—it all
comes together in The End. He proves he
may be one of the very few actors in films
with the talent, personality and range to
play the kinds of roles we now get to see
only on late-night movies.

Since Reynolds has so often been engagingly self-deprecating on talk shows about
his own performances, I have sometimes
wondered why he would keep harping on
critics for doing the same thing. Perhaps
he didn't think he was where he would
like to be in his career, and maybe he felt
the critical slings and arrows of outraged
reviewers were not aimed at his attempts
to act but at his attempts to survive. In
the closing moments of The End—when he
is screaming at God—you can almost sense
his own primal scream for the world to
pay attention and get off his back.

He no longer has to worry about survival, because with this film he has
arrived at wherever it is he wished his career to take him. For Reynolds, as an actor
and director, The End is a whole new
beginning—and no matter where he wants
that to take him, there are a lot of critics
who'll say, "Godspeed."

HOOPER

"Stunt men have the most exciting job in the movies. I wanted to do Hooper because it was about stunt men."

—B.R.

CREDITS

(Warner Brothers—1978)
Executive Producer, Lawrence Gordon; Producer, Hank Moonjean; Director, Hal Needham; Screenwriters, Thomas Rickman, Bill Kerby from a story by Walt Green and Walter S. Herndon; Cinematographer, Bobby Byrne; Editor, Donn Cambern; Art Director, Hilyard Brown; Set Decorator, Ira Bates; Music, Bill Justis; Assistant Director, David Hamburger; Special Effects, Cliff Wenger, Cliff Wenger, Jr.; Running Time, 99 minutes

CAST

Sonny Hooper, Burt Reynolds; *Ski,* Jan-Michael Vincent; *Gwen,* Sally Field; *Jocko,* Brian Keith; *Max Berns,* John Marley; *Roger Deal,* Robert Klein; *Cully,* James Best; *Adam,* Adam West; *Tony,* Alfie Wise; *Sherman,* Terry Bradshaw; *Hammerhead,* Norm Grabowski; *Bidwell,* George Furth; *Jimbo,* Jim Burk; *Sheriff,* Donald "Red" Barry; *Wanda,* Princess O'Mahoney; *Amtrac,* Robert Tessier; *Doctor,* Richard Tyler; *Debbie,* Tara Buckman; *Cliff,* Hal Floyd

Burt as Sonny Hooper in Hooper.

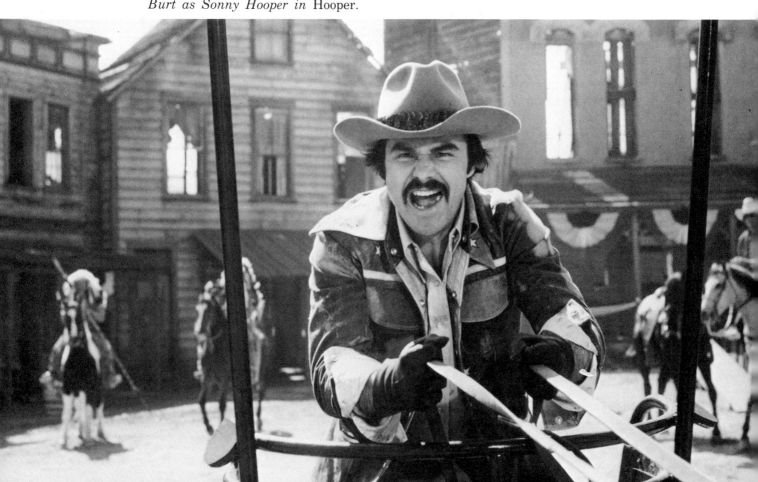

Charles Schreger—*Weekly Variety*—July 26, 1978

It's been too long since actors have projected as much on-screen chemistry as Burt Reynolds, Jan-Michael Vincent, Sally Field and Brian Keith do in *Hooper*. Individually, the performances in this story of three generations of Hollywood stuntmen are a delight. And Hal Needham's direction and stunt staging are wonderfully crafted. But it's the ensemble work of this quartet, with an able assist from Robert Klein, which boosts an otherwise pedestrian story with lots of crashes and daredevil antics into a touching and likable piece.

Reynolds, in a further extension of his brash, off-handed wise guy screen persona, plays the world's greatest stuntman. He took over that position 20 years back from Brian Keith. His status is being challenged by a newcomer, Jan-Michael Vincent.

To cement a place in the stuntman's record books, Reynolds must perform one last stunt, in this case a 450-foot jump in a jet-powered car over a collapsed bridge. He'll watch the gauges with Vincent behind the wheel. It'll be his final feat, and presumably afterwards, he'll hand over the reins to the next generation.

All this is to take place in a film, *The Spy Who Laughed at Danger*, some sort of a disaster James Bond–type picture being directed by the deliciously obnoxious Robert Klein.

The plot's elements have been dramatized before. Think of Sam Peckinpah's pictures about an aging hero performing one last heroic act to confirm his masculinity. But Needham, himself a former stuntman, and screenwriters Thomas Rickman and Bill Kerby have a sympathy for their characters—even Klein—rarely found in Peckinpah's pictures. And each of the performers displays an understanding and empathy not only for his own character, but also for each other's.

Sally Field plays Reynolds' girlfriend and roommate. This is her third picture opposite Reynolds and she proves again that she's one of the most reliable double threats working today—a capable comedienne who can switch mid-scene to serious drama.

Besides the final jump over the bridge, Needham and stunt coordinator Bobby Bass have arranged a smorgasbord of stunts—car

Sally Field, Burt Reynolds, and Jan-Michael Vincent.

"The greatest stunt man alive."

Burt leaps from a helicopter ...

... and continues his fall. After Burt's descent was filmed, the scene was enhanced by a record-breaking 257-foot fall performed by stunt man A.J. Bakunas.

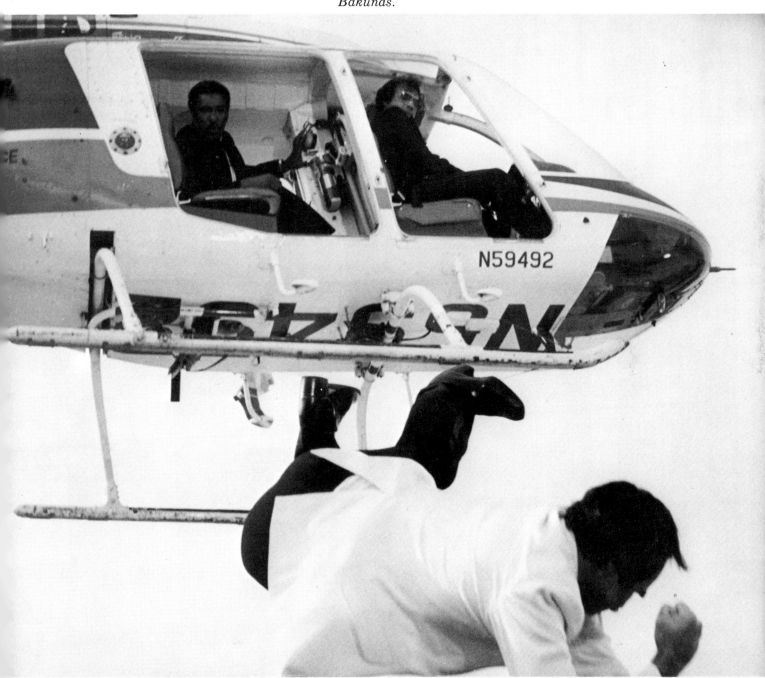

A little roughhousing—Burt, Terry Bradshaw, James Best, and Brian Keith.

Burt is hoisted and tossed by stunt man Tim Rossovitch.

Terry Bradshaw (extreme left, in striped shirt) ducks as Burt swings.

crashes, barroom brawls, chariot races, helicopter jumps and motorcycle slides. All are skillfully executed.

The question, of course, is, can Reynolds and Needham repeat the enormous success they enjoyed with *Smokey and the Bandit?* Because of the more serious overtones of *Hooper* and the film-within-a-film element, which has never been a big box-office draw, probably not. Still, outlook is big. The film will draw and please the action seekers as well as filmgoers looking for something more serious. And Reynolds continues to be one of maybe a half dozen dependable b.o. actors working today. His fans will flock to this one and not be disappointed.

Sally Field as Hooper's *best gal and James Best as his best pal.*

Director Hal Nedham gives final instructions to Burt before rolling a stunt scene; James Best, Jan-Michael Vincent, and Stan Barrett rest on the hood of an automobile.

Pittsburgh Steelers quarterback Terry Bradshaw makes his acting debut playing an off-duty policeman in Hooper.

Clint Eastwood and producer Lawrence Gordon drop by the set on Burt's forty-second birthday.

221

STARTING OVER

"I loved doing Starting Over. It was very close to the story of my life."

—*B.R.*

Phil Potter (Burt) is stunned when Jessica (Candice Bergen) asks for a divorce.

On his own in a strange city, Potter keeps making calls—but no one wants to go out with him.

CREDITS
(Paramount—1979)

Producer/Director, Alan J. Pakula; Coproducer/Screenwriter, James L. Brooks based on the novel by Dan Wakefield; Associate Producers, Isabel M. Halliburton, Doug Wick; Cinematographer, Sven Nykvist; Editor, Marion Rothman; Production Designer, George Jenkins; Set Decorator, Phil Smith; Music, Marvin Hamlisch; Assistant Director, Alex Hapsas; Running Time, 106 minutes

CAST
Phil Potter, Burt Reynolds; *Marilyn Holmberg,* Jill Clayburgh; *Jessica Potter,* Candice Bergen; *Michael (Mickey) Potter,* Charles Durning; *Marva Potter,* Frances Sternhagen; *Paul,* Austin Pendleton; *Marie,* Mary Kay Place; *Dan Ryan,* MacIntyre Dixon; *Larry,* Jay Sanders; *Everett,* Richard Whiting; *Barry,* Alfie Wise; *Jerry,* Wallace Shawn; *John Morganson,* Sturgis Warner

PICK OF THE CRITICS
Dale Pollock—*Daily Variety*—September 28, 1979

Starting Over is a delight. Much more than the flip side of *An Unmarried Woman,* to which it will inevitably be compared, the James L. Brooks production takes on the subject of marital dissolution from a comic point of view, and succeeds admirably. Wryly directed by Alan J. Pakula, and featuring an outstanding cast headed by Burt Reynolds, Jill Clayburgh and Candice Bergen, the Paramount Pictures release looks to be a box-office giant. In this instance, all the lucre will be well-deserved.

Brooks is the latest screenwriter to graduate from television sitcoms (preceded by Alan Burns with *A Little Romance,* among others), and the influence shows in some surprising ways. While there's a certain superficiality to *Starting Over,* it's more than balanced by the warmth and wittiness with

After much persuasion, Marilyn (Jill Clayburgh) becomes involved with Potter.

Marilyn follows Potter outside after a quarrel at her apartment.

Potter joins a divorced men's workshop. Clockwise from the top of the stairs: Alfie Wise, Wallace Shawn, Jay Sanders, MacIntyre Dixon, Richard Whiting, Austin Pendleton, Burt Reynolds.

which Brooks invests his characters, qualities Pakula so skillfully draws out.

In fact, *Starting Over* favorably evokes the screwball comedies of the 1930s in more subtle fashion than other pictures attempting to overly mimic the heyday of American screen comedy.

Success in this regard stems from a cast and concept wholly integrated. Reynolds plays a mild-mannered writer unwillingly foisted into a "liberated" condition by spouse Bergen, feeling her feminine oats as a songwriter. Fleeing to Boston and the protection of relatives Charles Durning and Frances Sternhagen, he meets spinster schoolteacher Clayburgh, and the off-and-on romance begins.

What brings the story alive is not just the preponderance of snappy one-liners, nor the sly way Pakula couples and uncouples his principal characters. Whatever their defects, Reynolds, Clayburgh and Bergen, along with the rest of the cast, are fun to watch. Audiences may wince at Bergen's

DIVORCED MENS WORK SHOP

autobiographical ditties, or shudder at Reynolds' misguided timing, but the essential link between comedy and reality is never absent.

Without his ever-present mustache, Reynolds is appealingly vulnerable, and in *Starting Over,* proves that he no longer has to prove anything. With unfailing comic timing and a superb sense of reaction, Reynolds is the core of the film, and underplays marvelously. It's a performance that should get the critics off his back once and for all.

Bergen hits a career highlight as Reynolds' slinky ex-wife, and her caterwauling voice provides some of the film's comic peaks. A perfect contrast to Bergen's chic profile is supplied by Clayburgh, looking purposefully blowzy, as a woman afraid of emotional entanglements, yet simultaneously yearning for one. It's a well developed character, right down to her apartment furnishings, and Clayburgh fleshes her out fully.

Director Alan Pakula, Jill, and Burt rehearse a Thanksgiving dinner scene.

Burt waits to be called for a scene filmed in a department store.

*Pakula, Reynolds, and Clayburgh stroll
down a picturesque street leading to
Boston's historic Quincy Market.*

Pakula is assumed to be a more serious
director than *Starting Over* would indicate,
but one of the film's strengths is its lack
of condescension toward its characters.
Even Durning and Sternhagen, both superb
as humanistic psychiatrists, are tweaked,
rather than ridiculed. Ditto for Mary Kay
Place, who is super as a man-hungry divor-
cee who literally attacks Reynolds.

The rest of the cast is likewise superb,
especially Austin Pendleton, MacIntyre
Dixon, Jay Sanders, Richard Whiting, Alfie
Wise and Wallace Shawn as members of
Reynolds' divorced men's workshop. Pakula
and Brooks are consistently able to turn
stock situations, such as this men's group,
into revealing and amusing insights, the
true mark of a film that cares.

Cinematographer Sven Nykvist, lensing
his first American screen comedy, has produced a warm, healthy glow well suited for
Starting Over, and George Jenkins, who

previously worked with Pakula on *All the
President's Men,* has provided the optimum
production settings. The rest of the credits
are all tops.

Starting Over is not without its over-
sights, clichés and lapses, but on the
whole, it's the most successful comedy to
come out after a long, mirthless drought.

Burt with his regular makeup man
Tom Ellingwood (left) and his regular
wardrobe man Norman Salling.

ROUGH CUT

"What I wanted to do in **Rough Cut** *was pay homage to Cary Grant. I tried hard. It didn't work."*

—B.R.

CREDITS

(Paramount—1980)
Producer, David Merrick; Director, Donald Siegel; Screenwriter, Francis Burns based on the novel *Touch the Lion's Paw,* by Derek Lambert; Cinematographer, Freddie Young; Editor, Doug Stewart; Production Designer, Ted Haworth; Set Decorator, Peter James; Music, Nelson Riddle; Assistant Director, David Tringham; Special Effects, Ted Grumbt; Running Time, 112 minutes

Burt Reynolds and Lesley-Anne Down.

Burglar Jack Rhodes (Burt) climbs to the third story of an English mansion and ...

... gets a surprise—someone is already stealing the household jewels ...

229

. . . so he leaves the way he arrived.

CAST
Jack Rhodes, Burt Reynolds; *Gillian Bromley*, Lesley-Anne Down; *Chief Inspector Cyril Willis*, David Niven; *Nigel Lawton*, Timothy West; *Ernst Mueller*, Patrick Magee; *Ferguson*, Al Matthews; *Sheila*, Susan Littler; *Inspector Vanderveld*, Joss Ackland; *Mrs. Willis*, Isobel Dean; *De Gooyer*, Wolf Kahler; *Pilbrow*, Andrew Ray; *Ronnie Taylor*, Julian Holloway; *Maxwell Levy*, Douglas Wilmer; *Tobin*, Geoffrey Russell; *Captain Small*, Ronald Hines; *Officer Palmer*, David Howey; *Passport Clerk*, Frank Mills; *Mr. Palmer*, Roland Culver; *Sir Samuel Sacks*, Alan Webb; *Mrs. Palmer*, Cassandra Harris

PICK OF THE CRITICS
George Anderson—*Pittsburgh Post-Gazette* —*June 23, 1980*

The scene is an elegant party in a stately English home. The formally attired guests wander through spacious rooms, carrying champagne glasses like talismans to ward off poverty. Bejeweled beautiful women mingle with decrepit old men, servants hover discreetly but usefully, inhibitions begin to weaken from the wine, and a dark, handsome, mustachioed man watches a glittering, slender, stunning young woman make her lone way through the crowd.

The man is not Cary Grant and the woman is not Grace Kelly—but it's the thought that counts.

That's good ol' boy Burt Reynolds inside that immaculate dinner jacket, but he knows what we're thinking. Minutes into the film when he first speaks, he delivers his lines in an impersonation of Cary Grant.

"That's the worst Cary Grant I've ever heard," says heroine Lesley-Anne Down.

"I wasn't doing Cary Grant," Reynolds replies. "I was doing Tony Curtis doing Cary Grant."

An inside joke inside an inside joke. Curtis did Grant in the classic *Some Like It Hot*, playing an imposter trying to seduce a beautiful woman. It's the sort of politely amusing business that helps make *Rough Cut* a cut above other summer comedies.

The film is a stylishly done caper-comedy in which even criminals have a touch of class. It's a clever career switch for

Reynolds, who proved again last year in *Starting Over* that he's capable of much more than playing rednecks. In *Rough Cut* he shows that he can handle literate dialogue in well-formed sentences as easily as he spouts CB jargon.

The new film is a revival of the gentleman-burglar sort of comedy. While it isn't as good as last year's delightful Sean Connery film *The Great Train Robbery*, also co-starring Miss Down, it is a pleasantly entertaining film nonetheless. It's even more welcome after the epidemic of hackneyed and acne-ed juvenile farces like *Up the Academy*.

Rough Cut gives us characters who know how to speak English, look clean, have reasonably civilized manners and, if they happen to be crooks, even manage to break the law tastefully.

Reynolds is Jack Rhodes, a former diamond thief who has always eluded Scotland Yard, much to the frustration of David Niven, who plays soon-to-be-retired Chief Inspector Willis. Willis would like to nab Rhodes in his last act, and he blackmails a socially high-placed kleptomaniac, played by Miss Down, to help him.

A $30-million diamond heist is placed temptingly before Rhodes, and the film's final half-hour sends the characters flying off to Antwerp and Amsterdam to pull off a fascinatingly planned robbery. Francis Burns' script has a neat twist at the end, a necessity for such entertainments. This one is deliciously ironic and satisfying.

Reynolds has a proven way with comedy, and he seems to relish the continuous banter of *Rough Cut*. The dialogue is what is usually called breezy, and if it isn't always as clever as it tries to be, there's enough droll humor to the piece to make it engaging.

Reynolds' blasé efforts to defend himself

Teaming up for a thirty-million-dollar diamond heist, Burt and Lesley-Anne disguise themselves as Arabs when going through customs at Antwerp Airport.

Scotland Yard's Cyril Willis (David Niven) drops in on Gillian Bromley and Jack Rhodes.

against an aggressively inebriated lady are quite funny. "You can have anything you like," she coos as she rips his shirt open. "How about a new shirt?" he asks.

Miss Down remains one of the most beautiful women in films, and her ladylike sexiness is in rare supply. Any movie becomes promising just by having her name in its cast. As for Niven, he is, of course,

The attractive thieves gather needed paraphernalia from Timothy West.

Mr. Reynolds and Mr. Niven—a mutual admiration society.

Rough Cut *stars Reynolds and Down—a smashing duo.*

one of the living masters at this sort of light byplay. His furrowed brow and quizzical look are treasures worthy of the British Museum.

The usually menacing Patrick Magee turns up quite hilariously as an unregenerate Nazi pilot who looks forward to flying over London again, although it won't be as much fun without bombs.

Rough Cut, which was produced by David Merrick, has the kind of attractively glossy look that makes it seem everyone and everything in the film has been varnished. The noted Freddie Young is responsible for the cinematography. The director, surprisingly, is Donald Siegel, best known as a top action director in the business because of his crisp no-nonsense films like *Escape from Alcatraz, Dirty Harry* and *Charley Varrick.*

Rough Cut looks and sounds exactly like a Blake Edwards movie, and Nelson Riddle has even managed to arrange Duke Ellington standards to sound like mellow Henry Mancini themes.

I found it all irresistibly mellow.

SMOKEY AND THE BANDIT II

"A bunch of good people got together again and had a good time."

—B.R.

CREDITS
(Universal—1980)
Producer, Hank Moonjean; Associate Producer, Peter Burrell; Director, Hal Needham; Screenwriters, Jerry Belson, Brock Yates from a story by Michael Kane based on characters created by Hal

Bandit and Frog—back together and on the road again.

Bandit—full of feathers, embroidery,
and himself.

235

Needham and Robert L. Levy; Cinematographer, Michael Butler; Editors, Donn Cambern, William Gordean; Production Designer, Henry Bumstead; Art Director, Bernie Cutler; Set Decorator, Richard De Cinces; Music, Snuff Garrett; Assistant Director, David Hamburger; Special Effects, Cliff Wenger; Running Time, 95 minutes

CAST

Bandit, Burt Reynolds; *Sheriff Buford T. Justice (Smokey),* Jackie Gleason; *Reginald Van Justice,* Jackie Gleason; *Gaylord Justice,* Jackie Gleason; *Cledus (Snowman),* Jerry Reed; *Doc,* Dom De Luise; *Carrie (Frog),* Sally Field; *Little Enos,* Paul Williams; *Big Enos,* Pat McCormick; *John Conn,* David Huddleston; *Junior,* Mike Henry; *Governor,* John Anderson; *Nice Lady,* Brenda Lee; *The Statler Brothers,* Themselves; *Fairground Owner,* Mel Tillis; *Don Williams,* Himself; *Terry Bradshaw,* Himself; *"Mean Joe" Green,* Himself; *Joe Klecko,* Himself; *Football Player,* Jeffrey

Charlotte picks Bandit up with her trunk and pitches him into a wooden crate.

Doc (Dom De Luise) and Bandit argue about Charlotte's delicate condition.

236

Bryan King; *Ramona*, Nancy Lenehan; *P.T.*, John Megna; *Everglades Attendant*, Dudley Remus; *Warehouse Guard*, Jerry Lester; *Gas Station Attendant*, Hal Carter; *Safari Park Attendant*, Rick Allen; *Party Guest*, Charles Yeager; *Ambulance Driver*, Patrick Moody; *Patient*, John Robert Nicholson; *Young Black Boy*, Anthony T. Townes; *Young Man*, Ritchey Brown; *Young Girl*, Nancy Lee Johnson; *Older Girl*, Gayle Davis

PICK OF THE CRITICS
Thomas Fox—Memphis *Commercial Appeal*—August 16, 1980

Smokey and the Bandit II isn't a sequel to Hal Needham's 1977 road comedy starring Burt Reynolds, Sally Field, Jerry Reed, Jackie Gleason, Paul Williams and Pat McCormick; it's a clone.

Following the theory that success is not to be tampered with, Needham has reassembled the old cast and poured them into a story little changed from the original. Once again, McCormick and Williams, as Big and Little Enos, hire Reed and Reynolds to haul something from one state to another. Last time, remember, 400 cases of Coors beer needed hauling from Texas to Georgia. This time, a pregnant elephant named Charlotte is being trucked from Miami to Dallas. And to adjust for three years of inflation, the prize money has been upped from $80,000 to $400,000.

Again, Miss Field gets dolled up for her wedding to Gleason's dim-wit son (Mike Henry); Gleason does several dozen slow burns and a lot of cussing while Reynolds speeds away in his black Trans Am. Reed drives the truck and plays the goodest of ol' boys. And Needham's background as a stuntman produces several spectacular chase scenes with a lot of fancy trick driving.

About the only major change in the cast is the addition of Dom De Luise as an Italian gynecologist kidnapped to nurse Charlotte through her labor pains. Gleason shines briefly while expanding to a triple role, playing not only Sheriff Buford T. Justice, but Justice's two brothers, Reggie and Gaylord.

To be fair, the story has been updated. Reynolds and Miss Field have broken up since the happy ending of *Smokey and the Bandit*, and when the Enos boys come call-

Burt, on his horse Cat Dancing, and director Hal Needham, on Burt's horse Dancer, mount up for a scene shot at the B-R Ranch in Jupiter, Florida.

In a high-risk stunt scene, Bobby Sargent and Janet Brady double for Burt Reynolds and Sally Field.

237

Burt's mom and dad, Fern and Burton Reynolds, visit their son during the filming of Smokey and the Bandit II.

ing with their deep pockets, they find him holed up in a roach motel, drunk as a monkey and moaning the loss of his image as a folk hero.

Fame, the kind that gets your picture on the cover of *People* magazine, has deserted him. His career as a singer resulted in the sale of a single record, and he hasn't been sober in at least a year. If there is a sub-

plot, it has to do with Miss Field attacking Reynolds' selfish ways until he realizes he really is a self-centered loudmouth.

Crude, mindless, scatological, foul-mouthed and happy, the film bounces along, grabbing every easy laugh and burning up enough diesel fuel to fill a supertanker.

THE CANNONBALL RUN

"Hal Needham kept telling me about this Cannonball idea. I kept telling him it wouldn't work unless he did this or did that—give this character an alter ego and get Dom De Luise to play it; and then get Roger Moore and have him play a guy who thinks he's Roger Moore. Before I realized it, I was really involved."

—B.R.

Burt as J.J. McClure in The Cannonball Run.

Cross-country racers Burt Reynolds and Dom De Luise.

CREDITS

(20th Century-Fox—1981)
Executive Producer, Raymond Chow; Producer, Albert S. Ruddy; Associate Producer, David Hamburger; Director, Hal Needham; Screenwriter, Brock Yates; Cinematographer, Michael Butler; Editors, Donn Cambern, William Gordean; Art Director, Carol Wenger; Set Decorator, Rochelle Moser; Music, Snuff Garrett; Assistant Director, Frank Bueno; Special Effects, Cliff Wenger; Running Time, 95 minutes

CAST

J.J. McClure, Burt Reynolds; *Seymour Goldfarb, Jr.*, Roger Moore; *Pamela Glover*, Farrah Fawcett; *Victor*, Dom De Luise; *Jamie Blake*, Dean Martin; *Fenderbaum*, Sammy Davis, Jr.; *Dr. Nickolas Van Helsing*, Jack Elam; *Mad Dog*, Rick Aviles; *Marcie Thatcher*, Adrienne Barbeau; *Shakey*, Warren Berlinger; *Stan*, Terry Bradshaw; *Jill*, Tara Buckman; *Subaru Driver 1*, Jackie Chan; *Bradford Compton*, Bert Convy; *The Sheik*, Jamie Farr; *Biker*, Peter Fonda; *Arthur J. Foyt*, George Furth; *Petoski*, Norman Grabowski; *Subaru Driver 2*, Michael Hui; *Sheik's Sister*, Bianca Jagger; *Van Driver*, Joe Klecko; *Mrs. Goldfarb*, Molly Picon; *David*, Mel Tillis; *Batman*, Alfie Wise; *Jimmy "The Greek" Snyder*, Himself; *Johnny Chan*, Johnny Yune; *Desk Sergeant*, Pat Henry

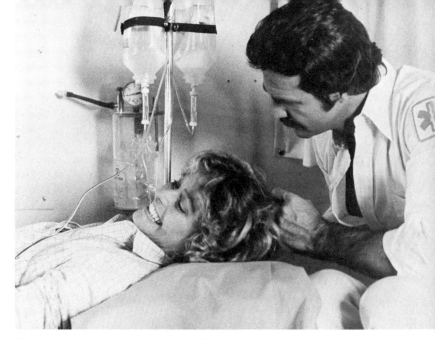

To gain an edge in the race, Burt impersonates an ambulance driver, and Farrah Fawcett is his make-believe patient.

PICK OF THE CRITICS

Frank Sanello—*Los Angeles Times*—June 21, 1981

More than any other film in recent memory, *The Cannonball Run* deserves to be judged by the values of the audience for which it was made: the drive-in movie crowd.

J.J. meets up with two priests (Dean Martin and Sammy Davis, Jr.) of a questionable order.

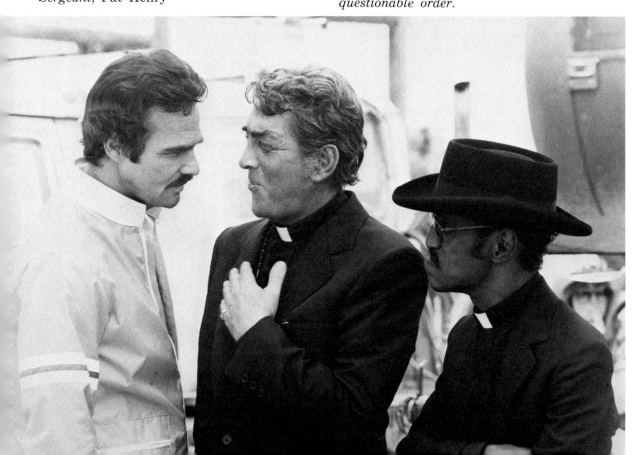

Burt with twenty-five—count 'em!—Cannonball extras.

As such, this latest Burt Reynolds vehicle—and the term can almost be used literally—may be the *Citizen Kane* of the good-old-boy-car-wrecking genre which began with *Smokey and the Bandit* in 1977. The plot and characters remain largely the same—only the make of cars and terrain have been changed.

This time around the speed track, the all-star cast is engaged in a cross-country race from Connecticut to California. The rules in this unintentional demolition derby are simple: there aren't any.

Based on a real life, biannual competition of the same name originated by screenwriter Brock Yates (some people will do anything to sell a script) and director Hal Needham, *The Cannonball Run* features a cast of zanies with all the depth of characterization of a Roadrunner cartoon.

The competitors in the race include Burt Reynolds, wearing his trademark "I'm-only-in-it-for-the-money" smile as auto mechanic J.J. McClure; mild-mannered sidekick Dom De Luise, who turns into superhero Captain Chaos when danger arises and the plot threads get tangled; and Farrah Fawcett as an ecologist with what seems to be a prurient interest in trees.

The funniest part belongs to Roger Moore's Seymour Goldfarb, Jr., heir to a girdle-manufacturing fortune, who suffers from the understandable delusion that he is movie star Roger Moore.

Farrari-driving Dean Martin and Sammy Davis, Jr., dress up as Roman Catholic priests and use their disguises to fool easily fooled highway patrolmen. (To paraphrase Blanche DuBois, the screenwriter apparently didn't want reality, he wanted improbability.) This duo's running—make that limping—gag as they ogle the gorgeous girls who decorate this film is to berate themselves for not choosing the alternate disguise of non-celibate ministers.

Jack Elam plays a crazed proctologist, hooked on drugs and egregious sight gags about what he likes to do with his index finger.

Supplying enough jiggle to cast several episodes of "Charlie's Angels" with some left over for a Benny Hill routine are Adrienne Barbeau and partner Tara Buckman, who manage to "charm" their way through a battalion of oversexed highway patrolmen until they meet up with a lady cop.

Jamie Farr's vulgar stereotype of an oil-rich sheik cries out for an Arab equivalent of the Anti-Defamation League.

Cameo appearances seem to have been expanded or contracted based on the box-office clout of the particular actor or actress: Bert Convy impersonates an Evel Knievel–type daredevil; Peter Fonda pays wistful homage to his *Easy Rider* biker role; Molly Picon resurrects the original Jewish mother (Seymour's, of course); Pittsburgh Steeler Terry Bradshaw wheels with Mel Tillis; Bianca Jagger as Farr's chic sibling has a one-line role and a gorgeous desert robe that looks as though it was designed by Adolfo; and Kung Fu movie star Jackie Chan kicks up a lot of dirt and even more Hell's Angels.

Character may have been destiny in Greek tragedy, but in *The Cannonball Run* the characters are the story—if you don't count the race, which seems to be little more than an excuse for mugging in front of the camera and demolishing enough cars to fill a used car lot in Long Beach.

If you are the sort of "consumer" whose idea of a good time at the movies is watching *Les Enfants du Paradis* without subtitles, pass on this one. But if your sense of humor tends to run toward the foot-in-cheek, get in the line which will inevitably form for Burt Reynolds' newest $100-million grosser.

PATERNITY

"Starting Over *was very close to the story of my life.* Paternity is *the story of my life.*"

—*B.R.*

CREDITS
(Paramount—1981)
Executive Producer, Jerry Tokofsky; Producers, Lawrence Gordon, Hank Moonjean; Director, David Steinberg; Screenwriter, Charlie Peters; Cinematographer, Bobby Byrne; Editor, Donn Cambern; Production Designer, Jack Collis; Art Director, Peter Smith; Set Decorator, John Anderson; Mu-

Burt as Buddy Evans in Paternity.

Burt Reynolds and Beverly D'Angelo.

Left to right: Norman Fell, Burt Reynolds, Paul Dooley.

sic, Dave Shire; Assistant Director, Benjy Rosenberg; Running Time, 94 minutes

CAST
Buddy Evans, Burt Reynolds; *Maggie*

Harden, Beverly D'Angelo; *Larry,* Norman Fell; *Kurt,* Paul Dooley; *Sophia Thatcher,* Elizabeth Ashley; *Jenny Lofton,* Lauren Hutton; *Celia,* Juanita Moore; *Tad,* Peter Billingsley; *Aunt Ethel,* Jacqueline Brookes;

Burt and Peter Billingsley take time out for some man-to-man conversation.

*Cabbie Alfie Wise picks up Manhattan
passenger Buddy Evans.*

Burt Reynolds and Lauren Hutton.

Left to right: Beverly D'Angelo,
Elizabeth Ashley, Burt Reynolds.

Cathy, Linda Gillin; *Tour Guide*, Mike Kellin; *Patti*, Victoria Young; *Prenatal Nurse*, Elsa Raven; *Ms. Werner*, Carol Locatell; *Claudia Feinstein*, Kay Armen; *Telegram Man*, Murphy Dunne; *Diane Cassabello*, Toni Kalem; *Laurie*, Kathy Bendett; *Teacher*, MacIntyre Dixon; *Cabbie*, Alfie Wise; *Butcher*, Tony Di Benedetto; *Mario*, Dick Wieand; *Falalfel Vendor*, Eugene Troobnick

247

Father-to-be Reynolds reads prenatal health instructions aloud as mother-to-be D'Angelo jogs through Central Park.

Robert Osborne—*Hollywood Reporter*—September 28, 1981

Burt Reynolds has a winner in Paramont's *Paternity*. It's a helium-weight comedy with Reynolds as a confirmed bachelor who is desperate to sire an offspring, and it plays beguilingly. The film was produced by Lawrence Gordon and Hank Moonjean (previous Reynolds collaborators) and it marks the debut of David Steinberg as a screen director. Box-office outlook: fertile.

Overall, *Paternity* plays for soft laughs rather than yuks. If the script by Charlie Peters is skimpy on hard plotting, it is nonetheless smoothly entertaining and rich in good-natured charm. At times the film also becomes as much an ode to the beauty of New York City as was Wood Allen's *Manhattan,* certainly the opposite end of the vision supplied by Sidney Lumet in *Prince of the City.* Fun City has rarely looked so appealing.

And, the bottom line—and perhaps the single most important aspect of the film—is the presence of Reynolds himself. *Paternity* doesn't stretch any of his acting muscles, but it does give good argument for those who consider him a screen presence strong enough to carry almost any script by sheer dint of personality. He is. He does.

Here, the premise is fun. Reynolds plays Buddy Evans, a supersuccessful New Yorker, manager of Madison Square Garden, who takes stock on his 44th birthday. "I'm a man who has everything," he reasons. "No wife, no house, no kids, no mortgage." But, before long, his best buddies (Paul Dooley and Norman Fell) insist he's missing out on the prime joy of existence: being a father. They tell him, "There's nothing to say Buddy Evans was here." Buddy is soon convinced.

Since he has no intention of giving up his single status . . . Buddy goes on the hunt for a woman by whom he can sire a child. Auditions go badly until, quite by accident, he meets a spunky waitress (Beverly D'Angelo) who needs some bucks to support a move to Paris, where she wants to study music. She doesn't want strings, either.

So far, so good. No emotion, they agree. With some awkwardness, they conceive. She begins the nine-month countdown, he continues dating other dollies (including Elizabeth Ashley, an old flame) and—no surprise to us—romance rears its head before the baby does. With that, *Paternity* rolls to an entirely predictable, entirely satisfactory conclusion.

Peters' script takes mighty good advantage of the situation at hand, nicely alternating between low-key interludes and more comedic situations, the latter which Steinberg directs with particular aplomb. . .t

Although Reynolds is the mainstay of the piece, *Paternity* offers topnotch performances down the line. D'Angelo takes another step up the ladder and makes a delightful partner and costar. Lauren Hutton, in for a bit as an interior decorator whom Reynolds mistakes as someone auditioning to have his baby, is the best she's yet been on screen. . .

The opening titles by Nina Saxon and Bob Hickson also deserve a mention: a montage of hooty baby photos, accompanied by a song called "Baby Talk" by Shire and David Frishberg (and sung on the track by Frishbert), finally drowned out by the wails of tots as the picture gets under way.

It's a terrific opening, and what follows never lets down.

249

SHARKY'S MACHINE

"When Clint Eastwood was going to make **Every Which Way but Loose,** *he sent me the script to read because he was a little nervous about doing comedy. I told him he was getting into my territory and if it was a success, I'd do Dirty Harry Goes to Atlanta. When he heard about* **Sharky's Machine,** *he sent me a telegram saying: 'You weren't kidding, were you?' "*

— *B.R.*

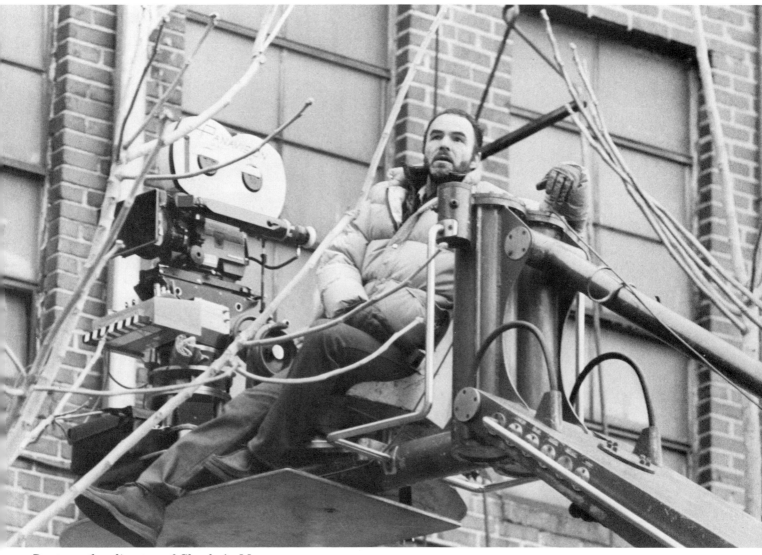

Burt as the director of Sharky's Machine.

CREDITS
(Warner Brothers—1982)
Executive Producer, Burt Reynolds; Producer, Hank Moonjean; Associate Producer, Edward Teets; Director, Burt Reynolds; Screenwriter, Gerald Di Pego based on the novel by William Diehl; Cinematographer, William Fraker; Editor, William Gordean; Production Designer, Walter Scott Herndon; Set Decorator, Phil Abramson; Music, Snuff Garrett; Assistant Director, Benjy Rosenberg; Running Time (unavailable at press time)

CAST
Sharky, Burt Reynolds; *Victor,* Vittorio Gassman; *Papa,* Brian Keith; *Friscoe,* Charles Durning; *Hotchkins,* Earl Holliman; *Billy,* Henry Silva; *Arch,* Bernie Casey; *Nosh,* Richard Libertini; *Dominoe,* Rachel Ward; *Smiley,* Darryl Hickman; *Joe,* Joseph Mascolo; *Highball Mary,* Hari Rhodes; *Siakwan's Man,* Val Avery; *Barrett,* John Fiedler; *Twigs,* James O'Connell; *Mabel,* Carol Locatell; *Siakwan,* Suzee Pai; *Tiffany,* Aarika Wells

Burt Reynolds and Rachel Ward.

Burt as the star of Sharky's Machine.

252

Burt and Earl Holliman. Friends for more than twenty years, both men own dinner theaters—Earl in Texas, Burt in Florida.

Trio of detectives—Brian Keith, Charles Durning, and Burt.

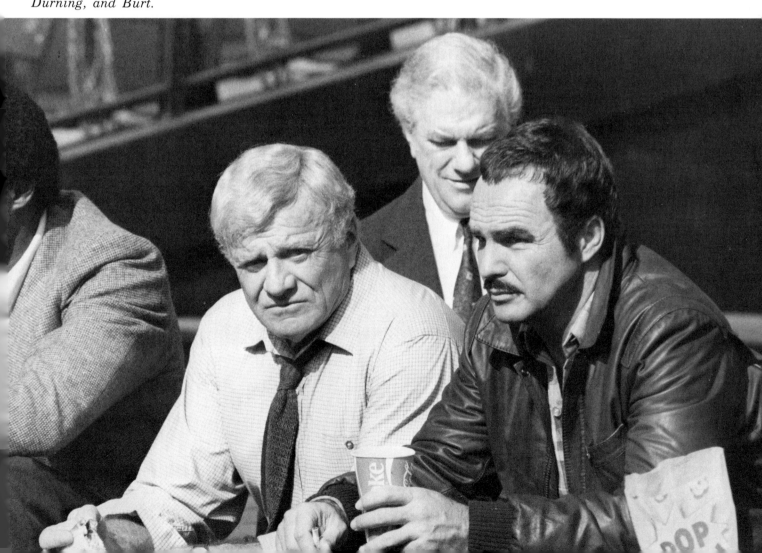

Left to right: Bernie Casey, Charles Durning, Brian Keith, Burt Reynolds.

The director and the cinematographer—Burt Reynolds and William Fraker.

Burt goes over a scene with Vittorio Gassman.

AFTERWORD

by Joe Baltake

Burt Reynolds remembers.

That's the large part of his appeal. He remembers what movies and movie stars used to mean to people. He remembers the simple, visceral pleasures of moviegoing of a bygone era, as well as the movie-fed daydreams and foolish fantasies that used to get us through life.

Somewhere in Riviera Beach, Florida, he was brought up on the notion that movies can influence a person's reality as well as his dreams. His life—his *art,* if you will—has been based strictly on movies, on vivid memories of Bogey in Rick's Café Americain and poor Bette Davis planting hyacinths while going blind.

His career—on screen, on film—beginning with his early penny-dreadful films and continuing with his more accomplished efforts in the 70s, has been an avowedly personal and joyful exploration of movies and movie images. In an almost kaleidoscopic way, his performances have recalled Cary Grant, Clark Gable, William Powell and Melvyn Douglas.

He's not so much a Movie Star—perhaps our last *real* movie star—as he is an amalgam of movie moods, movie styles and movie memories.

In a sense, he's a man, an actor, who's out of joint with his time. At a point in film history, when movies are either self-important or technological and when they *always* take themselves too seriously, we have Burt Reynolds, clinging to a personal conviction, a dream about what movies should be, and memories that he can't shake or forget.

He remembers. And to appreciate his screen work, you have to examine not his individual films, but the man, the image and the variation of performance that link them.

If you step back and observe objectively, you'll see that Burt Reynolds is about a dream—the American Dream, irrevocably tangled with the Hollywood Myth. In Burt Reynolds, on screen and off, we see an assurance of the good life and that it works. We see the fantasy of making it *big,* making it big in movies, becoming a star (a superstar even) but remaining unchanged.

He's bigger-than-life. Glamorous. Humorous. The Hollywood Myth of perfection. And yet, at the same time, he's incredibly simple and artless. The typical Burt Reynolds hero—be it in the cornpone *Smokey and the Bandit,* the urbane and criminally misunderstood *At Long Last Love* or the trendy *Starting Over*—goes down easy. Boyish and self-mocking.

His films may seesaw wildly in quality, but the charm, warmth and authentically individual vision that he brings to them link them.

This vision is contrary to the self-importance, technology and negativity that plague so many of today's movies. It's based on simplicity and optimism, on success tinged with innocence and humor. It's a vision that's largely unfashionable in these nihilistic times—and it's put a strain on Reynolds as an artist.

His fierce loyalty to his convictions, his dream, his image, and especially to the fans that relish that image, his desire to grow and evolve as a performer seem to have Reynolds caught up in a career whirlwind.

He'll go out on a limb with an *At Long Last Love* and he'll go against his natural ways in a *Starting Over.* He's always trying, stretching. He brings flair and feeling to just about everything he does, and even when he doesn't (*Smokey and the Bandit II* and *The Cannonball Run*), his performance makes it clear that, while he isn't stretching as an artist, he's attempting to please the crowd.

Few established actors are as sincere or work as hard as Reynolds. People like that. They've responded. This is a hunch, but I've a feeling that his fans know that his on-screen performances are colored by his off-screen personality.

It's exaggerated, of course, a lampoon, but there's probably some grain of truth to every woman's idea of Reynolds as macho perfection, every guy's idea of him as a great drinking partner and carouser, the talk-show image as a self-proclaimed, self-styled, self-satisfied star.

We've seen variations of these character traits in just about all of his films, with a touch of the big-brother-fighting-wrong-doings image in his good-old-boy flicks.

Burt Reynolds, in a nutshell, is the movie star who's a pal. "A wonderful partner," critic Molly Haskell observed in her review of the first film he directed, *Gator* (a film that's more sophisticated and complex than you'd think). "He is playful and quizzical."

But there's something else, something deeper, something sad that makes Reynold's playfulness and flippancy wrenching.

"There's some depth of feeling below his bantering," Pauline Kael noted in her critique of *Semi-Tough*. "Reynolds has timing. He's swift and cagey . . . [but] what makes it possible for him to hold the picture in his open palm is [his] hurting eyes."

That says it all.

In his eyes, we see Reynolds' integrity. They're what makes him an original in a business full of clones. We look at Reynolds and we see a man who's believed in old movies, the American Dream and loyalty; we look in his *eyes* and we see how difficult it's been.

Today's devoted film aficionados and even our critics can't fully appreciate what Burt Reynolds represents. Yes, he's out of joint. He may be too good for today's movies.

His secret with audiences is that he's one of us.